VIRTUAL REFERENCE SERVICE
from competencies to assessment

edited by R. DAVID LANKES, SCOTT NICHOLSON,
MARIE L. RADFORD, JOANNE SILVERSTEIN,
LYNN WESTBROOK, and PHILIP NAST

GW00371946

facet publishing

Published by Neal-Schuman Publishers, Inc.
100 William St., Suite 2004
New York, NY 10038

Library of Congress Cataloging-in-Publication Data

Virtual reference service : from competencies to assessment / edited by R. David Lankes ... [et al.]
    p. cm. — (The virtual reference desk)
   Includes bibliographical reference and index.
   ISBN 978-1-55570-528-2 (alk. paper)
1. Electronic reference services (Libraries). 2. Reference services (Libraries)—Information technology. 3. Electronic reference services (Libraries)—Study and teaching. 4. Reference librarians—Effect of technological innovations on. 5. Electronic reference services
(Libraries)—United States—Case studies. I. Lankes, R. David.
  Z711.45.V576 2008
  025.5'2—dc22
                                                    2008024104

*This book is dedicated to the vision and hard work
of Keith Stubbs.
Without his leadership, the Virtual Reference Desk
would not exist.*

.

Contents

Part I: Starting Up

List of Figures

Preface

R. David Lankes and Philip Nast

In the last decade, virtual reference has grown from a topic of largely theoretical conversation to a very real and increasingly basic library service. At the time of the first Virtual Reference Desk Conference in 1999, though excitement was high, there was no easy way for libraries to start a new virtual reference program. Those who had not been among the first wave of adopters had a hard time visualizing what exactly they were supposed to do. As the movement grew, software tools such as LSSI's Virtual Reference Toolkit and QABuilder were developed, allowing many more libraries to make the service a part of their institutions.

Today, libraries have a growing number of virtual reference options. Libraries can provide virtual reference by building a platform from scratch, using a specialized software package, or adapting a general tool such as instant messaging (IM). Precedents have been set for the legality of offering specialized medical and legal reference help. Problems unique to virtual reference, such as chat communication and inappropriate questions, are being addressed by serious researchers, and various solutions are being explored.

Virtual Reference Service: From Competencies to Assessment will likely be the last book to draw directly from the Virtual Reference Desk (VRD) conferences. As with past volumes in the Virtual Reference Desk series, the chapters included here, selected from the papers presented at the 7th Annual VRD Conference held in San Francisco, reflect the best of current research and practice. They represent the growing breadth and maturity of the virtual reference field. In addition, the chapters in this volume were chosen with an eye for work that will have particular relevance for librarians in years to come. Although this book serves as a capstone for the series, it focuses on the future, not the past.

Several chapters of *Virtual Reference Service: From Competencies to Assessment* address training as an issue that will have a great impact on the development of virtual reference. Chapter 9, "A Comprehensive VR Training Program," will be of particular interest to those involved in virtual reference training. In one of the Virtual Reference Desk's most ambitious projects, the Digital Reference Education Initiative spent three years developing educational competencies and standards for the field. "A Comprehensive VR Training Program," published here for the first time, is the culmination of this effort. We hope the skills and competencies described will become an integral part of both LIS courses that cover virtual reference and on-the-job training.

The theme of the 7th VRD conference was the evolution of virtual reference. It should come as no surprise that advancing technology continues to affect the way reference is practiced. As soon as libraries added e-mail reference to their menu of services, the appearance of instant messaging raised user expectations. Constant innovation and improvement, key for the continuation of any field, are especially important for virtual reference. The contributors to this volume are some of today's most creative voices in virtual reference. They are more than good researchers. They are librarians, academics, and others dedicated to making the profession-and the world-better.

Organization

Virtual Reference Service: From Competencies to Assessment begins with an introduction, "The Virtual Reference Desk Conferences as a Revelatory Case," giving a history of the seven VRD conferences and assessing their importance and legacy. The body of the book is divided into four parts, which roughly reflects the order in which libraries might encounter the topics covered.

Part I, "Starting Up," discusses the real-world challenges of implementing a virtual reference program. Chapter 1, "Creating Your Own Consortium in Less Than Six Months: A True Story of Virtual Reference," details how a committee with a tight deadline established a successful service in a group of 19 libraries across four time zones. Chapter 2, "Implementing VR on the Fly: Staff Motivation and Buy-In," shows that staff support for a new virtual reference program can be developed even in an environment of changing library leadership.

Part II, "Branching Out," goes beyond the basics to explore how libraries can expand existing programs and respond to new situations. Chapter 3, "Adding Instant Messaging to an Established Virtual Reference Service: Asking 'r u there?'" examines how libraries can most efficiently add chat-based reference services by discussing staff training issues and the pros and cons of different software packages. Chapter 4, "Responding to Triage Taxonomy: Answering Virtual Medical Questions," evaluates some existing taxonomies and proposes a "triage taxonomy," which might allow more libraries to provide health reference services by automatically distinguishing resource questions from diagnosis questions. Chapter 5, "The Evolving Role of Reference Librarians in the Health Sciences Environment," presents the current and possible future roles of the reference librarian and shows how librarians can effectively deal with the changing work environment.

Part III, "Ongoing Improvement," investigates ways in which libraries can make the virtual reference experience better for both users and staff. Chapter 6, "Examining Interpersonal Communication in Virtual Reference Encounters: The Library LAWLINE Consortium," identifies positive and negative communication behaviors in chat reference and recommends best practices for this unique communication environment. Chapter 7, "Assessing Inappropriate Use: Learning from the AskColorado Experience," provides answers to important questions about inappropriate virtual reference behavior: What are the trends? Have these trends changed over time? Does inappropriate behavior vary across markets?

Part IV, "Pulling It Together: VR Training," discusses how we can best prepare the library workforce to provide virtual reference services. Though the practice of reference has quickly adapted to technological change, chapter 8, "Meeting the Challenges of Reference Service in a Hybrid Environment: Teaching LIS Students Today," argues that library schools have been slow to follow suit. This chapter encourages educators to prepare their students for the realities of a mixed-service environment. Chapter 9, "A Comprehensive Virtual Training Program," answers the challenges presented in chapter 8 by providing a start-to-finish model for virtual reference training using the DREI competencies.

Virtual Reference Service: From Competencies to Assessment is the latest word on virtual reference from researchers and practitioners, but as the VRD conferences made clear, a library service so intimately tied to evolving technology will not remain unchanged for long. The community that formed at the conferences continues to grow and develop. We hope that the insights shared and questions raised in these chapters suggest new aspects of investigation for researchers and guidance for librarians in the application of virtual reference. Virtual reference is here. What will it look like in five years? In ten? We can only guess, but we are certain that the contributors to, and the readers of, *Virtual Reference Service: From Competencies to Assessment* will have an important role in the changes to come.

Acknowledgments

The editors would like to thank everyone who contributed to the planning and success of the 7th Annual Virtual Reference Desk Conference and to the development of this book. In particular, we would like to thank the conference sponsors: The U.S. Department of Education, Online Computer Library Center (OCLC), Syracuse University's School of Information Studies, and ALA Reference and User Services Association (RUSA). OCLC's George Needham, Nancy Lensenmayer, Donna Gehring, Mary Ann Semigel, David Nebbergall and Stephen Leonard deserve a special mention.

In addition, without those at the Information Institute of Syracuse—Blythe Bennett, Joann Wasik, and Joan Laskowski—the conference "Recognizing the Success of Reference" would not be possible.

Our thanks to the speakers, presenters, panel participants, and attendees, who all provided a valuable contribution to the conference and an ongoing dialogue.

Thanks also go out to the staff at the Information Institute of Syracuse and Neal-Schuman Publishers, in particular to Michael Kelley, the development editor, and Charles Harmon, director of publishing.

Starting Up

The Virtual Reference Desk Conferences as a Revelatory Case

R. David Lankes

This book is quite possibly the last in a series documenting work presented at the Annual Virtual Reference Desk conferences. The conferences, seven of them, were more than a simple set of events. They also set an annual agenda for the virtual reference community. They were structured as forums for practitioners and researchers to get together, share ideas, and identify areas ripe for investigation. They also were calling cards to the wider library communities. Through these books, online proceedings, new jointly funded projects, and invited guests, the conferences helped forge what Clifford Lynch referred to as a "movement."

It would be boastful and erroneous to say the series of conferences created the virtual reference movement. However, it is fair to say that these events helped bond, promote, and further the movement. Would virtual reference have gone from a series of disconnected experiments to a service staple in seven years without the conferences (see Figure I-1 for a description of the conferences)? It is impossible to say. What can be said, though, is that these conferences served as a center for the community, and therefore, a discussion of them is warranted.

In qualitative research, scholars talk about a revelatory case. These cases are important in that they reveal new information, often because the real-world phenomenon only recently has become available for study. With the ending of the U.S. Department of Education's support of the conference and the future of the event uncertain, the present seems a good time to reflect on the conference, its construction, intentions, and effects.

What follows is a case study of the conference. This case study has two purposes:

- to document the conferences for the historical record
- to provide future library "movements" with lessons learned

The intended audiences for this case, then, are two: those involved in virtual reference and future innovators seeking to change the library world. The

Figure I-1. Chart Summarizing VRD Conferences

#1	YEAR: 1999	PLACE: Boston, MA	THEME: Reference in the New Millennium	ATTENDANCE: 200

Virtual reference was new. There was a great deal of excitement on one hand and a great deal of concern on the other. Many libraries were still in the throes of adopting (and adapting to) the Internet collections and metadata, and the thought of re-examining reference was not seen as a positive activity in all corners. There was a fear that virtual reference would mean replacing trained librarians for other experts and AskA services. There was a concern about the role of help desks and new software in reference. For the most part, the community came together because of what virtual reference promised rather than to discuss its reality.

#2	YEAR: 2000	PLACE: Seattle, WA	THEME: Facets of Digital Reference	ATTENDANCE: 227

The feeling around the second conference was markedly different from the first. Rather than gathering out of fear of the unknown, the community came together excited to get involved. More of the attendees were now doing or starting to do virtual reference. There was a thirst for presentations with real services. While at the first conference participants crowded sessions discussing software, in Seattle they filled to overflowing every training session.

#3	YEAR: 2001	PLACE: Orlando, FL	THEME: Setting Standards and Making it Real	ATTENDANCE: 473

The general unease around the conference was related to a question of coherence. There were now a lot of experiments, but the question was, would services begin to standardize quality and technical standards. There were questions of sustainability. Many virtual reference services were started with LSTA grants, and their funding was finite. There was also concern that the emergence of chat reference might splinter the nascent movement.

Orlando also marked the end of the startup phase for the conference itself. The first three conferences had been organized primarily by the Information Institute of Syracuse with partnerships. Harvard and NELINET were the first partners in Boston. In Seattle the University of Washington helped organize the sessions and workshops. In Orlando it was SOLINET and Florida State University's School of Information Studies. All these partners brought their own skills, audiences, and perspectives to the conferences. All deserve a huge amount of credit for the virtual reference movement.

#4	YEAR: 2003	PLACE: Chicago, IL	THEME: Charting the Course for Reference	ATTENDANCE: 437

Chicago was different. For the 2002 conference, the Information Institute of Syracuse teamed up with OCLC. This had two effects. The first was the

(Cont'd.)

Figure I-1. Chart Summarizing VRD Conferences *(Continued)*

#4	YEAR: 2003	PLACE: Chicago, IL	THEME: Charting the Course for Reference	ATTENDANCE: 437

(Cont'd.)

deliberate effort to have each conference set and continue an agenda. Rather than being a simple forum for news and research, the conference was now an ongoing conversation. The program was put together to identify trends, and an ending session was set up to capture and check emerging trends at the conference. Also, the beginning of this and each subsequent conference would now track and report trends from the former conference. Eric Jewel of OCLC deserves much of the credit for this new element. The end result of this approach was a series of community-wide initiatives like the Digital Reference Education Initiative, the NISO AZ technical standards process, and the creation of quality standards and measures.

The second effect of partnering with OCLC was that the conference became more professional. George Needham and his team made the Virtual Reference Conference not only interesting to attend, but fun. The food was better, registration easier, and the locations more interesting. There was some initial concern that partnering with OCLC might lead to bias or preferential treatment for OCLC products such as QuestionPoint. However, George was adamant that this would not be the case.

Virtual reference services bordered on mainstream and still had a sort of an "in" glow. In four years, the movement had gone from having to lobby to try virtual reference in their libraries to explaining why they didn't have a service. Chicago also started asking the question "Is virtual references any different from reference?" Some said "We never had a conference for phone reference." Joe Janes put it best when he said the true sign of any successful service is the dropping of a modifier—virtual reference to reference, digital library to library and so on.

#5	YEAR: 2003	PLACE: San Antonio, TX	THEME: The Reference Roundup	ATTENDANCE: 314

The question of a difference between virtual reference and reference in general was taken up by the organizing committee of the San Antonio conference that now included representatives from ALA's Reference and User Services Association. The question was how to balance the reality that virtual reference and face-to-face reference services were merging with the overwhelming feedback from conference goers that the value of the VRD conferences were their focused presentations. The conclusion was to include sessions on the merger of virtual and traditional reference and to make part of the conference agenda about how to guide this merger.

It might not have been hostility so much as bravado, but there was an increasing sense on the part of the virtual reference movement that it must change traditional reference. The hidden agenda of the movement—to

(Cont'd.)

Figure I-1. Chart Summarizing VRD Conferences *(Continued)*				
#5	YEAR: 2003	PLACE: San Antonio, TX	THEME: The Reference Roundup	ATTENDANCE: 314
(Cont'd.)	increase the technical and innovative capacity of reference librarians—had become more obvious. The conference goers also become more specialized. Whereas Chicago has seen a mix of first-time attendees and regulars, San Antonio was more of a meeting for active virtual reference types.			
#6	YEAR: 2004	PLACE: Cincinnati, OH	THEME: Creating a Reference Future	ATTENDANCE: 250
	Cincinnati saw the continued evolution of the virtual reference community. Notably, there was a lot of discussion about merging traditional reference and virtual reference and the incorporation of new technologies into virtual reference. The international flavor of the conference also expanded.			
#7	YEAR: 2005	PLACE: San Francisco, CA	THEME: Virtual Reference Evolution	ATTENDANCE: 271
	San Francisco, as it stands, was the last of the VRD conferences. At the end of the conference, it was announced that the Department of Education would no longer be continuing the project, and OCLC—their staff already over extended—simply could not do it on their own resources. However, after a call for help, there has been regular discussion among the virtual reference community in bringing the conference back. Stay tuned.			

latter of these two is of particular importance. Innovation in practice, re-search, and intellectual grounding is essential for the continuation of any field. Today, when libraries, once the cornerstone of information in an infor-mation-poor environment, are facing challenges in a now information-rich environment, new thinking is crucial. The only means to continued relevance is the perpetual re-examination of current practice, continual attempts to identify new practice (both from within and without the profession), ongo-ing reevaluation of the profession's core values (to bolster those still mean-ingful and reject the outdated), and a ruthless disregard for business as usual. The point is *not* that only new things are valuable but that age does not equal merit.

This is a continuous state of reflection and action. Note that these two aspects must be joined. Reflection without action is paralysis and reification. It is research and theory without grounding. It is hypothesis without data. Action without reflection, on the other hand, is random. It is practice without research, a sort of frenetic attempt at the new without any concept of the better. If there is one thing that should stand out from the Virtual Reference Desk conferences, it is that the marriage of reflection and action is possible, not accidental.

Lesson 1: The Difference between the Content of Research and the Business of Research

Before any specific discussion of virtual reference, it is important to set a context. Virtual reference is a relatively well-examined field. Through proceedings and books, as well as academic journals and conferences, answering questions online has been well explored. From transcript analysis and system design to user surveys and case studies, a great deal is known. This large body of research constitutes a rich source for knowing the "why" of virtual reference. What is missing from this corpus is the "how." That is, how has virtual reference moved from a few disconnected experiments to a movement and what are the tactics and strategies in cohort building and getting the library community's attention?

If we label the overall endeavor of investigating a phenomenon, such as virtual reference, as research,[1] then the "why" questions can be labeled as the content of research. The content of research is emphasized in library schools and among scholars. It deals with good research questions, valid methods, solid links to theory, and so forth. It is the basis of any good innovation. The business of research, on the other hand, takes good ideas and uses them to garner greater attention and resources. It is the project management behind a good study, a dissemination plan after the final chapter is written, and an implementation plan after the data has been analyzed.

Many people conflate these two aspects, content and business. Many believe that having a good idea is enough. It is not. "If I'm right," or "if I am brilliant," or "if the need for this is obvious then it will get funded/done/talked about/cared about," is merely a belief. It is all too true that the best ideas never get traction without a champion, as well as care and feeding. It may seem mercenary to say that promoting an idea is as important as developing it, but that would be missing the essential importance of dissemination. The very act of taking an idea, however well examined, into the marketplace of ideas and practice is an essential part of the investigative loop, and it too has methods. These methods are not as well examined or as rigorous as methods of inquiry, but they are not to be dismissed lightly. As has been repeatedly shown in the communications literature, a good message is easily lost through bad communication.

A Special Note to Academics

It is often uncomfortable to talk about the business of research. We are trained, and rightly so, in the content of research. One risks being thought an opportunist or dismissed as a salesman instead of a serious scholar by talking too loudly about this issue. This is a mistake. The mistake is twofold: It misin-

---

[1] This is a purposefully broad use of the term research. Many might break this down into categories such as applied and basic research; some might reserve the term for only scholarly investigations. While each of these distinctions is important, in the context of this discussion they are not helpful.

terprets a focus on business as a substitution for content, and it negates the inherent value of validating content in a practice community. Let's take these in turn.

Let me state again that the business of research is no substitute for the content of research. Further, the business of research is going to be very different in manner and degree across the spectrum of research activities. It may mean nothing more than getting good ideas published in reputable journals. It may mean recognition from a relatively small peer group. However, for good ideas to have effect, some effort to disseminate those ideas is needed. The "publish or perish" reality of today's academy is recognition of the business of research concept.

The second mistake is to regard the time spent in promoting ideas (be it in the market of ideas or in an aligned professional community as exists in library science) as wasted time. Taking the time to apply research is seen as beyond the duties of the academy. Worse, it is often considered that applying research provides no new knowledge to the research itself. This is certainly not a universal view. Boyer has spent considerable time refining the concepts of scholarship to include the scholarship of application and teaching to the scholarship of discovery. It is worth restating the value of these scholarships here and talking about research as a cycle of practice and discovery.

Working in a practice community, like librarianship, one has an opportunity to draw empirical data from real practice, as well as an opportunity to validate results in real life situations. Figure I-2 outlines this cycle of practice/research participation. Note the similarities to grounded theory development and the lessons learned from action research.

It should be noted that this simple figure does not attempt to capture the complexity of the practice/academy relation. It does not, for example, show knowledge coming from within the practice community and/or outside the field altogether. Rather, this high-level view attempts to capture the reason for continuous involvement with the community of practice. Working directly with practitioners identifies new practice, sources of data, and the outstanding needs of the community.

The implementation phase—the hallmark of the business of research—adds a new level of validity to social science research and theory. In the messy real world where many variables interact, implementation and the readiness of a practice community to adopt a given idea is a holistic means to test theory against reality. It provides scale to your work. It is direct proof of the universality or transferability of one's research.

Lesson Conclusion
Virtual reference is a good idea, and it has been well researched. There is a great deal of solid research on how virtual reference is done, how librarians perceive virtual reference, and how users perceive the service. If nothing else, virtual reference has, to a degree, revitalized research in reference of all sorts and refocused reference from collections and materials to people and services.

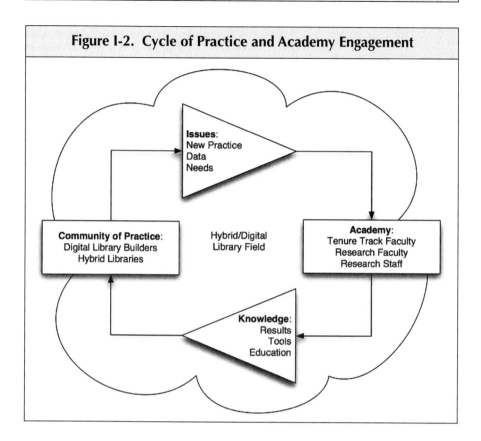

Figure I-2. Cycle of Practice and Academy Engagement

However, there is a difference between the research on virtual reference and the story of how virtual reference went mainstream. The story of its adoption by the library community is the business of research. The business of research in virtual reference was to take an innovation and turn it into an accepted practice in the library community. This, then, is a further refinement to the focus of this case study: lessons on the business of research for innovators.

Lesson 2: The Importance of Tools

The Virtual Reference Desk began as the Digital Reference Resource Development project in 1996, as a special project of the ERIC Clearinghouse on Information & Technology funded by the U.S. Department of Education. The project also received support from the White House Office of Science and Technology Policy. The purpose of the project was to build on the success of AskERIC and the MAD Scientist Network in other educationally relevant topic areas. In short, to build a cohort of so-called AskA services that could enrich classroom learning.

The project benefited greatly from strong champions within the U.S. Government. Blane Dessy, Director of the National Library of Education, Keith

Stubbs, Director of the ERIC program, and Kirk Winters in the Secretary's office were largely responsible for creating and funding the project. Kirk and Keith served as guardian angels for the project during its nine-year history and deserve an immense amount of credit for the current state of virtual reference.

The project, renamed the Virtual Reference Desk Project, spent its first years developing resources such as:

- The AskA Starter Kit: A workbook that discussed the steps needed to set up a virtual reference service, from planning to training to prototyping to evaluation. The book was published as an ERIC monograph and focused on building services for education.[2]
- AskA Digests: Short, one-page briefs on a virtual reference topic, such as question submission forms and the state of AskA services in science. These topics were often used to build partnerships.
- The AskA+ Locator: An Internet portal to virtual reference services useful to the K–12 community. Users could search for AskA services by topic or name.
- Virtual Reference Network: A network of AskA services like AskERIC, the Internet Public Library, Ask A MAD Scientist, and others that exchanged questions. Questions were sent from one service to another to better match scope (topic area) and scale (if a service had too many questions).
- Facets of Quality for Digital Reference Services: This document grew out of the Virtual Reference Network and outlined criteria a service must meet to participate in the network.

By the end of the startup phase, the Virtual Reference Desk had gained a lot of insight into how digital reference services should be built, developed a cohort of AskA services, and established contact with possible builders of so-called AskA services. What it didn't have was a new service created by industry or organizations. It made several attempts to reach out to industry, with mixed results. The biggest lesson learned from this startup period was the importance of tools.

The pattern became familiar. The VRD team would present to an interested audience. The organization would love the idea and ask "so how do we get started." The answer, ultimately unsatisfactory, was "Go build a service." Even though the AskA Starter Kit went into great detail about starting a service, the hesitancy to begin was always for the same reason—there was no easy means of implementation.

This is not to say that these organizations were somehow lazy. Virtual reference was new. Those who had not been among the innovators of the service

---

[2] It was not widely adopted in the library world because it did not specifically address how libraries and librarians could build a virtual reference service, even though it was more a matter of different terminologies used by the education and library communities. Call it a mini lesson that tight communities like librarianship are more likely to adopt tools that use their own terminology.

had a hard time visualizing what exactly they were supposed to do. They needed clear and immediate guidance. While this could be provided in many forms, including in-depth consulting, the most efficient way was to provide a tool. In the case of virtual reference, it was a piece of software.

The importance of tools in advancing innovation is nothing new. The World Wide Web, for example, had been developed more than a year before wide-scale adoption. The first great push was not, as many have said, Mosaic, a graphical browser, but NCSA HTTPD. HTTPD was an easy-to-compile Web server. It made providing content via the Web relatively easy. Once there was a supply of compelling content available for Mosaic to browse, adoption of the Web skyrocketed. The point is that though Tim Berners-Lee provided a great idea, the standards, and ideas of the Web, it took a tool that made these obvious for the innovation to take hold.

The same can be seen in the virtual reference community. As will be discussed, there was a great deal of interest in virtual reference before there were many virtual reference services. It took tools like those provided by Collaborative Digital Reference Service (CDRS—later QuestionPoint), 24/7 Reference, and LSSI's Virtual Reference Toolkit to allow virtual reference to succeed in libraries.

It is interesting to note the current trend away from digital reference packages to more open and general tools like Instant Messaging (IM). There are two possible explanations for this trend. The first is that these general tools have become "good enough" to support virtual reference, or perhaps more likely, the virtual reference community has become comfortable enough with virtual reference that they no longer need the confines of specific tools. In either case, the necessity of tools can still be seen.

Beyond virtual reference, the need for tools to build a movement and advance innovation is still in play. Certainly the types of tools also will become more varied. In research, it might be a method complete with research instruments (surveys, formulas, etc). In some areas of librarianship, it might be classifications documents and standards (like MARC and AACR2).

Tools are a double-edged sword, however. On one hand, they present a vision of how an innovation can be implemented. On the other hand, tools also encompass other less obvious messages to potential users. From preconceived notions about innovators, the crafting skills of the tool builders (e.g., the coding skills of a programmer), and the limitations of current technologies, tools can alienate just as easily as they entice. A few examples will help illustrate this point.

Take the current crop of commercial virtual reference solutions. They certainly do the job, and yet they have become increasingly similar. Who determined that a chat window scrolling down the right hand side of a screen with a large area for pushed pages on the left is the optimal configuration for reference? Many have commented that easily sent "scripts" have made it easy for librarians to sound like robots. Take a careful look at these tools and you will see a way to do virtual reference, but only one way.

Lesson Conclusion

To conclude this lesson, we need to jump ahead a few years to the development of QABuilder by the Virtual Reference Desk project. QABuilder was a hosted application that allowed anyone to quickly create an AskA service through a Web interface. Now, when VRD talked to organizations interested in setting up a virtual reference service, they could do it in 10 minutes. The service has been used in several projects, from East Asian Language groups, to AskA services for the disabled, to the National Science Digital Library. Are there better tools available? Yes. The point is that there are now tools available. Tools helped push virtual reference from a conversation to a reality. QABuilder became a new research instrument where people could see virtual reference in action. Abstract concepts and ideas (such as triage and question acquisition) also became concrete. The creation of tools not only made the content of research real in practice, but raised a host of new research questions.

Lesson 3: Build on Existing Communities

It might have come to the attention of the reader that the Virtual Reference Desk project did not start out as one focused on libraries. The focus in the first years was on content organizations and K–12 education. Why then did the Virtual Reference Desk Conference become a library conference?

The leap from education to libraries is not much of one. The project was part of the National Library of Education, the funded organization was Syracuse University's School of Information Studies that housed the library science program, and most of the initial staff had advanced degrees in librarianship. The conference focus on libraries was partly missionary zeal, partly crass practicality, and partly an emergent (and troubling) trend. The zeal was the desire of the VRD team to promote librarians in whatever they did. The practicality is the point of this lesson.

In the spring of 1999, virtual reference was being talked about in library circles. Joe Janes and the Internet Public Library deserve a great deal of credit for demonstrating the reality of virtual reference and for training a dedicated band of librarians through their service. A year before, the Library of Congress had hosted an institute on "Reference Service in a Digital Age," and Diane Kresh and Linda Arrett of LC were laying the foundations of what would become the Collaborative Digital Reference Service. In California, Steve Coffman and Susan McGlamery were deep in the development of 24/7 Reference. These same names seemed to come up again and again on panels and at events. What if they all could be pulled together in a single event?

At the same time, the Virtual Reference Desk project was preparing an annual meeting of its network. It was going to be at Harvard's Graduate School of Education, which just happened to have a conference center as part of the Gutman Library. Why not add on a day-long conference for folks in the area? John Collins, the director of the library, was extremely helpful and supportive in doing this. The VRD team also approached NELINET, an area library consortium that also thought it was a great idea and really made the conference a reality. In the space of a few months, the first Virtual Reference Desk Conference was on. It was a great success. Conference attendees had to be limited to 200 participants, and a daylong workshop was added on the second day. The conference covered its cost and ended in the black, a somewhat rare achievement for the first year of any conference.

So why the history lesson? The conference simply could not have been pulled off in the education community. It needed the existing community infrastructure that the library community possessed. NELINET not only knew how to put on events, but had the mechanisms to take participant fees and get the word out. Harvard not only had the space, but had the staff to handle meeting logistics. It is somewhat ironic that the feature that many in libraries point to as an inhibitor of innovation, namely the overabundance of associations, organizations, and consortia, can play such an instrumental part in disseminating new ideas. The lesson learned here was that using existing infrastructures and building within existing communities of practice can be easier than building new structures. In fact, many within these organizations are hungry for new ideas and will advance innovation when it aligns with the more personal mission of advancing the profession.

So now, let's address the unexpected and somewhat troubling trend that resulted from our choice to use an existing community. The first VRD conference at Harvard had a very diverse set of attendees. By far the largest were librarians. However, there were AskA services, government representatives, and industry players as well. The first awards given at the conference went to Remedy Corporation, a help desk software vendor, and to exemplary AskA services like IPL, MAD Scientist Network, and the like. By the third conference, a non-library attendee was a rare exception.[3]

The virtual disappearance of the AskA community at the conference and on the DIG_REF listserv was noted in a VRD Consortium meeting. A library colleague mentioned that this was not the first area with which he has been involved where librarians have pushed out other stakeholders. Upon further reflection, this is exactly what had happened. The conference had become increasingly geared to the library community in terminology and outreach. Part of this was due to the need to meet market demand, and part was the simple fact that, while AskA services still existed, the growth in terms of numbers and sophistication was happening in the library world. Yet ultimately, the inability to reach other communities (like the K–12 education field, the computer science community, the search engine community, and the help desk community) was a failure of the conferences. Call this a corollary to the lesson: Building on existing communities can jumpstart the adoption of innovation, but at some point that community may well reassert traditional boundaries.

Lesson Summary

The library community is rich in structures that can be used to jumpstart innovation. While some may see the abundance of consortia and associations as a hindrance, there often are elements of these organizations that are inclined toward innovation. However, as was demonstrated by the virtual reference movement's insular reaction to AskA services, innovation within a community may be easier to promote than expanding a community through partnering with related communities. Community boundaries of language, membership, credentialing, and culture can be hard to penetrate from the outside and may push out innovators who cannot adapt to the establishment.

Lesson 4: Building Zip Cords between the Towers and the Trenches

In Lesson 1, the interplay between the academy and practice was discussed. The conclusion was that scholars and practitioners need each other. This is far from a revolutionary idea. The question becomes how to motivate the two communities to interact. Some academics get it. Some in practice get it. But the necessity is not always apparent to all. There is a prevailing tension between librarians and library science faculty. Sometimes this is seen in the context of accreditation, the library versus information "word" debate, and sometimes in the everyday discourse of conferences.

The point is that when the two communities work together, the results can be impressive. Practicing librarians bring real services to real people. They make local connections to resources and service populations. Academics can bring reflection, prototypes, national-level funding, and prestige to local communities and community leaders. In order for these two vital groups to work together, the VRD conferences built a suite of incentives. For academics, VRD became a clearinghouse of ideas, a quick matchmaking service between communities with real needs, funders seeking real solutions, and researchers with the skills to bridge the two. The VRD conference proceedings became a reviewed outlet. For practitioners, the conferences provided hands-on examples, a chance to meet with vendors (both formally and informally), a chance to network, and, most importantly, a chance to participate on a national stage.

Lesson Summary

The result of this deliberative structure of academics and practitioners was a community created on the basis of ability to collaborate and demonstrate real value in real services, rather than that of status or home institution.

Conclusion

The Virtual Reference Desk conferences were successes. While each had its distinct flavor, the conferences as a whole served as milestones for the power of an energized innovator community. What you see in these pages and the pages of the previous VRD volumes are more than good research or case studies. What you see are librarians, academics, and others dedicated to making the world a better place.

This community has been accused of being more interested in technology and myopic in terms of other concerns in running a service, but nothing can be farther from the truth. This community has developed strong evaluation instruments, solid empirical research, and a body of good work. What's more, this community gathered annually to work across boundaries and egos with the express purpose of putting better information into the hands of the user regardless of time or place. While barriers were discussed, they were never used as excuses. No one ever introduced themselves by saying how long it had been since they received their library degrees. This was a band of dedicated problem solvers. Everyone in the movement should feel a great sense of pride in their work.

Chapter 1

Creating Your Own Consortium in Less Than Six Months: A True Story of Virtual Reference

Helene Lafrance, Locke Morrisey, and Judy Trump

Overview

When the Association of Jesuit Colleges and Universities (AJCU) launched its own virtual reference service with 19 participating libraries across the country, they charged an implementation committee to:

- select virtual reference software (Tutor.com)
- organize individual institutional online training
- write policies and procedures
- develop a 24 hour schedule across thee time zones

The committee addressed major issues, including:

- the reluctance to change to different software by those institutions already offering a reference chat service
- the lack of buy-in from all participants
- the failure of some to foresee benefits of virtual reference provided by a consortium versus on one's own

The project produced two major learning lessons:

- always create and maintain good communication channels among members
- always maintain excellent relationships with the software provider

The committee also developed and implemented a model to ensure quality control. The chapter concludes by presenting the results of a six-month post-implementation survey among member institutions and various possibilities to improve service and ensure long-term success.

Introduction and Background

The Association of Jesuit Colleges and Universities (AJCU) includes 28 institutions that share a common vision but operate independently. Over the years, the libraries have worked on a few collaborative projects mostly related to collections, such as interlibrary loan agreements and reciprocal borrowing. During their annual meeting, the library directors discussed the possibility of offering a collaborative virtual reference service. They first appointed a task force charged with evaluating software. When the task force came back with their recommendations in April, a six-member team charged with implementing a collaborative virtual reference service was appointed. The mandate was simple: Make this happen by the start of the Fall semester, about six months away! This article highlights the trials and adventures of the implementation team members as they negotiated the contract and service agreements, struggled to organize training for librarians across the country, developed policies and procedures, and prepared a schedule among libraries in three time zones.

After a few days of sheer panic following the announcement of the short timeline, the members of the implementation committee got down to work. They soon discovered that there was a fair amount of literature on various aspects of virtual reference, but very little on collaborative service. In fact, in an article on the trends in digital reference research published in 2005, David Lankes identified policies and standards for digital reference in consortium as an area of needed research (Lankes, 2005). A few articles, however, proved to be very useful; one on the implementation of the Ohio Link consortium (Webb and Barr, 2003) and another on quality standards for virtual reference consortia (Kasowitz, Bennett and Lankes, 2000). Other than that, the committee charged ahead, reading, learning, and solving problems as they emerged.

Choice of Software

When the implementation committee began its work, the software had already been selected by the previous task force that had reviewed and evaluated several products before deciding to go with Tutor.com. The criteria for software selection were determined by the type of service AJCU wanted to offer—the around-the-clock service appropriate to their academic clientele. The co-browsing function of the software was deemed essential in order to be able to teach how to use the databases. Also, a company offering evening and night services on a contractual basis was needed. After narrowing down the choice to four candidates (24/7 Reference, Tutor.com, QuestionPoint, and Docutek), Tutor.com was selected unanimously. Not only did the company have software that met the requirements, but it also offered a contractual service and a lower price quote.

Implementation Committee

The implementation committee appointed by the AJCU library directors included six librarians representing the various geographic locations of the Jesuit institutions. Two members who had served on the task force that selected the software were named co-chairs. This continuity made it easier to ensure uninterrupted communication with Tutor.com. The committee members, none of whom were given any release time to complete this colossal project, did all the preliminary work by email, phone, and fax. All of the members worked closely together, but the committee soon divided the work among three teams: The co-chairs focusing on contract negotiations and development of policies and procedures; another team taking over training and scheduling; and the last group concentrating its efforts on marketing.

Details of Implementation
The following describes the initial steps taken by the implementation committee. These were not necessarily sequential steps. It was realized early on that all these things had to happen simultaneously in order for the project to be implemented in time.

Contract Negotiations
One of the first tasks of the committee was to negotiate with Tutor.com to come up with a contract that reflected the diversity of the consortium and at the same time was fair to the smaller institutions. In order to streamline the process, one contract was negotiated for the consortium as a whole, rather than as 19 individual contracts. Legal review of the contract was conducted by the Georgetown's Office of the University Counsel and accepted by all participating libraries. We agreed on three cost tiers for the different institutions determined by the size of their undergraduate student bodies, and although there was only one contract, Tutor.com agreed to bill the institutions separately, based on the information provided by the steering committee.

Determination of Individual Institution's Commitment
Before the drafting of a schedule could begin, agreement had to be reached on the number of hours each institution would contribute to the consortium. The committee decided on three tiers: The larger institutions would provide 10 hours of coverage a week, the medium ones seven hours, and the smallest only four. The AJCU librarians would staff the virtual reference service from 10 a.m. to midnight (EST). The remaining hours would be covered by the contractual service (called Librarians by Request), as stipulated in the contract with Tutor.com. After determining the extent of each institution's commitment, the director of each library signed a Participation Agreement, which detailed their obligations to the consortium.

Communication Channels
To ensure the success of the project, each participating library was asked to appoint a Virtual Reference coordinator who would be in charge of the service locally. The role of the local coordinator was essential to the success of the project, especially because a decision was made early on that some of the functions of the project would be decentralized as much as possible. Local coordinators

would bear the full responsibility for organizing training locally, developing a policy page and a Web entry page for the service, marketing the service, and overall championing the project among their staff. A listserv was created to share all the administrative information with the local coordinators. Later on, a second listserv was set up for all the librarians providing the service.

Software Training

All software training sessions, for administrators and providers, were done online during the summer. Needless to say, it was a challenge to make sure that at least one member from every single institution attended a session. Tutor.com was very cooperative during the entire process and offered enough choices of training dates to satisfy everybody. Most institutions chose to offer the training in a classroom setting where several librarians could participate simultaneously. At the same time, Tutor.com had to work with the systems person at each institution to ensure the compatibility of the software with local electronic resources.

Policy Pages

Each participating institution was asked to develop a policy page according to a pre-established template. This policy page makes it easier for librarians from other institutions to answer institution-specific questions. It provides quick access to the library's important phone numbers, circulation policies, list of databases, research guides, etc. (For examples of policy pages, see: www.library. georgetown.edu/ajcu_vr/participants.htm.) Most of the policy pages are hosted at Georgetown University on the site specially designed for this project.

Policies and Procedures

The implementation committee created a "Service Policies and Guidelines" document providing an overview of the service, performance standards, guide-lines regarding scheduling and quality control, use and privacy policies, and duties of participating institutions. Each institution was asked to read and review the document which is available online at: www.library.georgetown. edu/ ajcu_vr/index.htm.

Scheduling

Two members of the committee concentrated their efforts on preparing a schedule for the service. The challenges were multiple: Institutions had different time commitments, the consortium initially covered three time zones, and the consortium was planning on covering 11 hours a day with AJCU librarians. The scheduling process was decentralized as much as possible. A scheduling software was selected (WhenToWork.com), and a template including all the shifts to be covered was created. To decide how many librarians needed to be online at certain times of day, the committee used statistical data from three institutions which had previously offered virtual reference services. Although not perfect, this strategy proved to be rather accurate over time. When the template was ready, the Virtual Reference (VR) coordinators were provided with detailed instructions regarding the number of hours (business and non-business) they were asked to cover, and shifts were selected online. This did not go as smoothly as expected, and one member of the committee spent a significant amount of time resolving scheduling conflicts.

Access to Databases

It was determined early in the project that it was essential for the virtual reference providers to be able to direct students to the resources available at their own institutions, whether the online catalog, the periodicals list, or any proprietary database. The use of proprietary databases in a consortial environment raised some issues related to licensing agreements. To avoid licensing infringement, it was decided to always have the patron authenticate the use of proprietary resources. In other words, if an AJCU librarian were helping a student from Georgetown University and wished to show him how to use one of Georgetown's proprietary databases, the student would be asked to authenticate himself in order to access the database. The librarian then could co-browse with the student and instruct him or her in the use of the database. Each institution was asked to provide a dummy login and password to allow participating librarians access to each institution's databases in case legitimate users were having problems authenticating. These logins and passwords were available to the Librarians by Request staff and the AJCU librarians staffing the service, but were to be used only as a last resort.

Marketing

After debating the choice of a name for the new service, the committee decided once again to decentralize the process. Although the AJCU library directors would have preferred a common name highlighting the collaborative venture, many institutions already had been offering virtual reference services of some kind under their own "brand" name. The local coordinators thought it would be really difficult and counterproductive to change the name of the service just as patrons were getting used to it. The AJCU logo would be featured on the patron's entry page for the service, but each institution would have its own name: Ask a Librarian, Live Help 24 × 7, Chat with a Librarian, Live Chat, Get Help!, AskLive, AskUs!, etc. Therefore, each local institution was responsible for designing materials and marketing the service to its community. The implementation committee did create guidelines and a list of suggestions on the best ways to highlight the service and increase use.

Quality Control

The importance of quality control in a consortium environment cannot be emphasized enough. Many institutions are reluctant to join a virtual reference consortium because of their concerns about the quality of service to their patrons. Some of the AJCU libraries were part of other consortia before joining the project and were not satisfied with the quality of the past service. Therefore, the AJCU implementation committee put together a simple quality control program before the start of the service. A quality coordinator was appointed, and a section on quality control was incorporated in the "Service Policies and Guidelines" document. Individual coordinators were strongly encouraged to review the transcripts involving their patrons and their librarians, as well as the survey responses from their library's patrons. They were asked to forward any problem transcript to the quality control coordinator whose role was to act as an intermediary. After receiving a complaint, the coordinator followed up with the librarian involved in the VR session. When the librarian involved was a "Librarians by Request" staff member, he followed up with their supervisor.

Problems and Challenges

Amazingly, all the above tasks were completed in a timely manner, and the service was officially launched. The "amazing" part was due to the fact that the odds of starting a consortium in less than six months were definitely against us. In a 2003 article entitled "Consortia and Their Discontents," Thomas Peters listed the 12 major discontents engendered by consortia, with "time delays" being number two on the list. "Although the wheels of academe turn slowly, incredibly, the wheels of consortia turn even slower" (Peters, 2003: 111). Things can drag on forever when you need to share information or obtain permission from 19 institutions before moving on any aspect of the project. This project's success was most likely due to the fact that it was a relatively small consortium. There was, of course, some confusion in the beginning, with dozens of questions being asked daily on the coordinators' listserv, but overall the first few weeks of service went rather smoothly. Nothing was perfect though, and over the next few months, the committee identified several problems.

One of the problems was the lack of motivation at some of the participating institutions. One has to remember that the project was mandated by the group of library directors, and that the frontline librarians were not necessarily consulted. In many cases, the librarians—who had to provide the service—were not "sold" on the project, to say the least, and just saw it as an additional burden. In other cases, some of the libraries had been using another virtual reference software package and were unhappy about having to switch to a new one. The benefits of the advanced features in the Tutor.com software such as the co-browsing function, and the advantages of a collaborative service which allows us to offer around-the-clock service to our patrons had to be repeatedly emphasized to ensure cooperation.

Some problems were difficult to resolve because they were not really within the consortium's control. Problems with the software, for example, emerged early. The co-browsing function did not work consistently, and the number of disconnected sessions was alarmingly high. In addition, the software was not Macintosh-friendly and had other compatibility problems with some browsers. These technical problems increased the frustration of some of the librarians providing the service. Tutor.com claimed that all the glitches would be corrected in the next version of the software, which was not really a satisfactory answer.

Despite efforts to pass along all new information to consortium members, a survey distributed to librarians after six months of service revealed that communication remained a problem. The use of two separate listservs might have been confusing to people, and coordinators might not have passed on all the information to new librarians. Resending information about different aspects of the project several times during the year turned out to be a better approach. The implementation committee also decided to take advantage of national conferences, such as American Library Association (ALA), Association of College and Research Libraries (ACRL), and Virtual Reference Desk (VRD), to organize informal meetings among members in attendance. The idea was that face-to-face meetings would enhance communication and increase enthusiasm for the project.

Creating a satisfactory schedule for the AJCU consortium proved much more difficult than anticipated. As mentioned before, members were given instructions on how to use the scheduling software and a date to begin choosing their shifts. People who waited too long were left with less desirable shifts and were very vocal about their dissatisfaction. The software was also somewhat confusing because it only displayed in Eastern Time. Those from the west coast or the central states had to do some quick mental calculations every time they looked at the schedule. In truth, the scheduling process was not completely fair because of the geographic distribution of the consortium, with the majority of institutions located on the east coast. In order to be able to staff the service with AJCU librarians until 9:00 p.m., the three west coast institutions were asked to contribute more evening hours.

Another problem that has been overlooked was the difference in the academic and holiday schedules of each institution. Each time a holiday came around, many institutions notified the consortium that they would be closed and unable to staff their shifts. Christmas, Easter, and the various semester and spring breaks turned out to be a scheduling nightmare. Even though each institution had the opportunity to post shifts for trade on the WhenToWork Web site, it was very difficult to trade during breaks and holidays. Many times, Tutor.com's contractual service was asked to take over during those periods despite concerns that the increase in the numbers of hours they covered would affect the renewal cost of the contract. In addition to all the problems mentioned above, the consortium also had to face unexpected events, like reassigning shifts after the closure of Loyola New Orleans following Hurricane Katrina. One way to improve the scheduling process would be a more flexible contract with Tutor.com where their contractual librarians would take over automatically when AJCU librarians could not cover their shifts. Of course, such flexibility would come at a cost.

Finally, despite the fact that a quality control program was in place from the start of the project, some participants still were dissatisfied with the quality of service received by their students. The problem was that they did not routinely follow the process and forward the bad transcripts to the quality control coordinator. At this point, because we did not have a full-time, dedicated coordinator for the consortium who could spend time reviewing transcripts, the success of the quality control program depended on the commitment of individual institutions. If local coordinators did not review the transcripts weekly, for lack of time or interest, there was no way to ensure consistent quality.

Assessment

To evaluate service, the consortium studied use statistics, customer surveys, and a provider survey that was distributed after the first six months. Looking at the statistics for the first year of service, the service was judged as very successful. The service answered an average of 686 questions per month for a total of 9,050 transactions. Sixty-six percent of the questions were answered by AJCU librarians and 34 percent by the contractual service. Most institutions have reported a slow but steady increase in the number of questions asked by their patrons, but the use is still very uneven among the various libraries. Georgetown University's patrons, for example, use the service more than anybody else, while some of the smaller institutions have very low usage. There might be different reasons for that (previous use of a virtual reference service, university culture, presence of distance education programs), but low use seems to be linked directly to the marketing efforts of the local institution and the number of access points for the service.

At the end of each virtual reference session, patrons were asked to answer a few questions in an exit survey. The compilation of these customer surveys showed a high level of satisfaction. In fact, the average satisfaction value based on all questions was 6.06 on a scale of 7 (highest) to 1 (lowest).

After six months, a survey was distributed to all librarians involved in the project. The level of satisfaction with the service provided was definitely not as good as what was hoped for. Many librarians reported resistance and a mixed level of support for virtual reference on their campuses and stipulated that it would take them more time to adjust to virtual reference. Several expressed their frustration with the shortcomings of the software, complained about the scheduling process, and wished for better communication among AJCU coordinators, librarians, and Tutor.com. When asked how virtual reference compared to traditional reference service, most felt that virtual reference was inferior to traditional reference and that VR worked well for ready reference questions but not as well for in-depth research questions. The results of this survey put a damper on the enthusiasm of the implementation committee, but at the same time gave clear indications of what the priorities should be in order to improve the service.

A Year Later

The AJCU consortium renewed its contract with Tutor.com after a year of service, and this time the terms allowed for more flexibility regarding the coverage by the contractual service. Of the 19 participating Jesuit institutions, only one wanted to withdraw because of lack of use and participation on its campus. They finally decided to stay for one more year but were expected to leave at the expiration of this year's contract. Four new institutions joined the consortium, including one more from the west coast and one from the mountain time zone, which should allow for more flexibility in the schedule.

After the service's first year, the coordinators from 23 institutions involved finally met face to face for the first time at Georgetown University for a very productive meeting. Over a two-day period, the coordinators discussed a wide range of issues, from governance and scheduling to marketing and quality control. The whole group reviewed policies and procedures and wrote guidelines for the election of a steering committee that would gradually replace the implementation team members. What emerged clearly during the meeting was the need for a permanent (and paid) coordinator who could dedicate his time to the success of the project and take over some of the most demanding tasks, including contract negotiations and scheduling. Common sentiment was that the sustainability of the project was in danger without a dedicated coordinator, even on a part-time basis. In the article previously cited, Peters's warning was clear: "People who participate in consortial activities are dedicated, busy professionals. Maintaining the interest, energy, and momentum of a disparate group of people is difficult, especially when the activity is not their day job" (Peters, 2003: 111). A proposal was made to the library directors to fund at least a half-time coordinator position, along with continuing efforts to hire a paid coordinator. Until that happens, the new steering committee will need to continue holding the fort.

During the Georgetown meeting, Tutor.com presented the newest Tutor.com software release. This new version of the software was expected to solve some of the technical glitches of the previous version and improve statistics capabilities. The consortium was excited about this new development, although plans for additional training had to be made.

With the service solidly in place, it is time to reflect on the learning experiences and focus on future service enhancements. Starting a virtual reference consortium was not an easy task, but despite the problems and glitches, the consortium's patrons have benefited tremendously going from limited or no virtual reference capabilities to round-the-clock service. Collaborating with colleagues from other Jesuit institutions has also been enlightening and rewarding.

References

Kasowitz, Abby, Blythe Bennett, and R.D. Lankes. 2000. "Quality Standards for Digital Reference Consortia." *Reference & User Services Quarterly* 39, no. 4 (Summer): 355–363.

Lankes, R. David. 2005. "Digital Reference Research; Fusing Research and Practice." *Reference & User Services Quarterly* 44, no. 4 (Summer): 320–326.

Peters, Thomas A. 2003. "Consortia and Their Discontents." *Journal of Academic Librarianship* 29, no. 2 (March): 111–114.

Webb, Kathleen M., and Belinda Barr. 2003. "Implementing Virtual Reference for OhioLink: 79 Peas in a Pod." In *Implementing Digital Reference Services: Setting Standards and Making it Real*. Edited by R. David Lankes. et al. New York: Neal-Schuman.

Chapter 2

Implementing VR on the Fly: Staff Motivation and Buy-In

Clara Ogbaa, Lorin Flores Fisher, and Lisa Ancelet

Overview

Over the past few years, academic libraries around the country have been expanding reference services to include virtual reference in order to meet the needs of a growing new generation of students. Members of the academic community now regularly conduct research from their computers, anywhere and at any time. In spite of this fact, it continues to be a colossal challenge for academic libraries to establish effective virtual reference services to serve this population. There is more to planning virtual reference service than making a "to do" list. Questions to be answered are:

- What are the keys to thinking with a specific goal in mind?
- How to develop a plan to reach that goal?

Staff motivation and buy-in serve as the foundation for implementing a successful virtual reference program.

Introduction and Background

All virtual reference projects are pilot projects. None of us yet have got it figured out.

(Coffman, 2003: 21)

Rapid changes in the library world have been extensively documented in the literature in the past 20 years. Fear of change is a large obstacle to success in implementing new services, but libraries must do so in order to remain relevant to users, especially younger generations. Much has been written on adapting library services to meet the needs of these Web-user generations who come to the library with a radically different mindset and service expectations than previous generational cohorts (DiGilio and Lynn-Nelson, 2004; Gardner and Eng, 2005; Lippincott, 2005; Sweeney, 2005). There are various reasons why there is so much difficulty implementing change. The culture of an institution may discourage change (Sweeney, 2005: 173). Also, a library workforce encompasses different generations of workers who may differ in how they respond to and approach change (Lancaster, 2003). Given that the pace of change in this work environment is constant and rapid, having a strategy to guide staff through transition and change is an essential management skill.

Chat reference is a relatively recent development in library services and represents another method to meet patrons on their own turf. This service has been around for close to 10 years. Early adopters of chat reference now have established services, and their combined experiences and research have enriched professional journals. However, even well-established services can suffer from issues arising from low staff morale and can benefit from renewed motivation or face discontinuation of the service (Horowitz, Flanagan and Helman, 2005). Chat reference is still not as common as e-mail reference, especially for smaller or rural institutions that have taken a little more time to migrate certain services online. For those who haven't yet joined the first wave of chat reference, motivating staff and encouraging staff buy-in are extremely important for a smooth implementation. If planned well, with a positively motivated staff, implementation of chat reference can be accomplished so swiftly that it is virtually an on-the-fly implementation. The case of the Albert B. Alkek Library illustrates an example of a targeted chat implementation focusing on staff motivation and undertaken rapidly.

Over the last few years, Texas State University-San Marcos, Texas (Texas State) has experienced immense growth. Texas State's current enrollment is 27,171 students in 115 undergraduate programs, 84 Master's programs, and six Doctoral programs, with more under review for addition. In comparison, enrollment in 1995–96 was 20, 917 students. In addition, the university is undergoing a cultural transformation from a Master's-granting institution to a Doctoral-granting research university. A significant number of students and faculty commute to the campus from surrounding cities. Along with continued growth at the main campus in San Marcos, Texas State also offers distance education programs online and off-site. For example, Texas State offers several programs at the Round Rock Higher Education Center (RRHEC). This multi-institution facility is about 50 miles away from the main campus and offers students living in North Austin and Williamson County an opportunity to attend classes closer to home without the long commute.

As the university grew, and its image changed from a small regional university to a larger, culturally diverse campus, so has the Albert B. Alkek Library. Many of the changes the Alkek Library experienced are due to technological advancements over the last decade, which often occurred quickly. The Alkek Library is the main library on the Texas State campus. Its collection currently contains over 1.5 million volumes and approximately 150 online databases. The Library is a selective federal and state document repository and also houses the Southwest Writers Collection and Witliff Gallery. At present, 11 full-time Reference librarians serve an ethnically diverse, mostly commuting student body at all levels of their education. Additionally, the RRHEC campus has a satellite library, staffed with one reference librarian and a library assistant, serving students from all the partner schools offering classes at that location.

Changes at the Alkek Library have paralleled trends occurring in the wider world. Since the debut of the World Wide Web in the early 1990s, changes included migration from legacy, standalone systems to CD-ROM to full-text online database, as well as journals and books with access available from any Internet connection (Coffman, 2003: 9). Traditional face-to-face reference services and print resources began to lose their luster and effectiveness with patrons. For example, reference desk statistics fell steadily at the Alkek Library, from 90,885 requests in 1992–1993 to 21,354 requests in 2004–2005. As many other libraries have witnessed, Alkek experienced increasing numbers of remote users as library resources migrated online. This trend is expected to continue due to younger students' increasing comfort level with technology and their tendency to prefer finding things on their own (Sweeney, 2005: 170–172). More and more of university's students use the Internet as an information-seeking tool and visit the physical library less. To meet the needs of the growing online community, the Alkek Library began offering e-mail reference in 1999.

Before Virtual Reference: A Traditional Management Model

The reference department underwent a major shift when the department head retired after 30 years of service. The management structure was traditional in nature, with library administration at the top and mid-level managers at the departments, followed by staff. The reference department was arranged military style, with irregular communication (Lancaster, 2003: 36). Reference service innovations were initiated from the bottom and moved up, as permitted by management.

Customer service was a priority under the previous department head, and external customer satisfaction ratings indicated a high level of customer satisfaction. Although the department was well-liked, staff often experienced less overall satisfaction because of resistance to change, either in growing new services or allowing older services to evolve fully. Despite the fact that over the last decade the Alkek Library had expanded its electronic collection to over 150 databases, added thousands of electronic journals, and launched its fifth-generation Web site, the previous manager felt more comfortable with traditional print resources and face-to-face services. Management philosophy and style directly affected service development and staff motivation. It was in this atmosphere that virtual reference (VR) was originally investigated but was not implemented. Those involved in the research decided it would be best to wait for a new department head before pursuing it again.

Embracing Change: Rethinking Common Goals

The arrival of a new department head presented an opportunity to implement radical change. The department as a whole wanted to take a more active role in developing cutting-edge services for users, and especially to target the under-graduate population mostly made up of those who entered school in the new century. Echoing a tendency noted in Barr, Conley and Goode (2003), the library had been unconsciously following a version of the Kano model (based on Total Quality Management principles) for measuring customer satisfaction. Virtual reference seemed an obvious candidate as a promising beginning by introducing a new "excitement feature" (Barr, Conley and Goode, 2003: 21). The new ser-vice hopefully would address a need that the customers were not consciously aware of and would appeal to users familiar with chat in their daily life. It also would serve the distance learning population and give those students an easier method to get help remotely (Kern, 2004). Virtual reference was envisioned as a new layer of reference service, not a replacement for traditional reference. However, before the initial planning stages for VR, a new service philosophy needed to lay the foundation for an effective and swift implementation.

Essentially, the reference department adopted a version of the Total Qual-ity Management (TQM) "inverted pyramid" (Waldman, 1994: 41). In this model, management hierarchy is upended, with customers, including external and internal, or staff at the top. This is similar to the "flattened pyramid" pro-posed by Jan Carlzon (1987: 59–74). Carlzon's concept of "moments of truth" was also vital to the adoption of a new emphasis on customer service (Carlzon, 1987: 59–74). To accomplish the change, staff needed to update and acquire new skills and competencies. Management took a more active role in providing support, training, motivation, and better communication. Many TQM concepts already adopted in the library were re-emphasized, such as the concept of continuous improvement and that of intensive training and retrain-ing (Masters, 1996).

The first task in planning the pilot VR project involved generating staff consensus. Through individual consultations and department meetings, the de-partment head identified people who liked change and encouraged them to participate in the planning. This was an essential step for implementing change (Mendelsohn, 1998: 43; quoted in Green and Chivers and Mynott, 2000).

A taskforce of 10 library staff members from the Reference and Computer Information Services departments convened to investigate VR issues, such as staffing models, consortiums, funding, software, marketing, and training.

The charge for the taskforce read as follows:

- to develop the virtual reference pilot project plan for the Alkek Library by investigating and evaluating products on the market for VRS
- to assess the appropriateness of each of the products for the library and users and make recommendations concerning software selection and in-tegration with other platforms
- to provide an implementation strategy for the Fall semester, including timeline, and identify resources needed, such as staffing and funding

Research of the VR literature revealed an important component for suc-cess: Active participation of all staff whose workflow will be impacted by adding another layer to existing reference service (Stemper and Butler, 2001; Ward et al., 2003). This process included soliciting feedback to all suggestions in all phases of the planning and implementation. Taking time for feedback helped ensure a successful execution of the pilot project. Once the task force identified five potential software vendors, reference staff attended the demonstrations and offered additional feedback. Staff was also included in other tasks, such as creating policies, staffing practices, and marketing the pilot project.

Another important factor was training. Proper training raises staff competencies, skills and increases the comfort levels of all reference staff (Coffman, 2003: 58). Some of the methods included internal reference workshops in customer service, best reference practices, and intensive onsite training by the VR vendor. The department also arranged a two-week timeframe before the go-live date. During these two weeks, VR practice was scheduled for all librarians and staff. Once the pilot project began, frequent in-house refresher training was provided when requested.

Incorporating trust in a working environment is a significant factor affecting buy-in for a new service. A non-threatening, non-judgmental workplace encourages staff to be more accepting of change and receptive to new services and changes in workload. Equitable distribution of VR hours—an average of one hour per day per staff member—did not increase workload to a great extent. During the pilot, librarians logged in from their office without the interruptions that might have occurred at the main reference desk. The schedule was flexible, and two dedicated VR reference librarians provided backup for multiple patrons and technical problems. At first, these dedicated librarians logged on alongside the other scheduled librarians. Later, as comfort levels increased, they logged in only when needed.

Although the project had the cooperation and participation of librarians, another critical factor in the success of the Alkek Library's VR pilot project was buy-in from upper management. Besides adding VR to the annual performance appraisals of all reference librarians, management also approved the hiring of a VR librarian to coordinate and manage the new service. These additional human resources increased the chances of success. Material resources included high-quality technical support for VR software and hardware. Intrinsic resources involved the motivation generated by the involvement in the process and intensive training. Performance recognition was achieved by developing a culture of celebration within the department and the library. Recognition of VR librarians for excellent service from patron feedback, division accolades, and commendations for good work at Library Council and reference department meetings all supported this new culture.

Researching the process helped Ask a Librarian Live to be a successful pilot project, which has evolved into a permanent reference service for all of Texas State University students, faculty, and staff. Additionally, including the reference staff in the research, setup, and go-live process made the transition to a new service more acceptable to them because there was not a moment of surprise. Staff had a year to work on their virtual reference skills and to familiarize themselves with the idea of continuing the service on a permanent basis. The statistics for VR have continued to increase, more than tripling in live chat and e-mail since beginning the service in the Fall of 2004. It is evident the service has enhanced the institution's traditional reference services.

Conclusion

An effective motivational strategy that fosters staff buy-in and maintains high morale and energy substantially eases the introduction of new services, especially in cases where an institution wishes to implement on a fast track. The Alkek Library's experience has revealed another factor that contributed to the success of its pilot project: An emphasis on virtual reference as an enhancement or extension of reference service went a long way in helping staff overcome negative feelings.

References

Albert B. Alkek Library. 1992. *Annual Report for Fiscal Year*. San Marcos, TX: Southwest Texas State University.

Barr, Belinda, Jerome Conley, and Joanne Goode. 2003. "Chat Is Now: Administrative Issues." *Internet Reference Services Quarterly* 8, no. 1/2: 19–25.

Carlzon, Jan. 1987. *Moments of Truth*. Cambridge, UK: Ballinger.

Coffman, Steve. 2003. *Going Live: Starting & Running a Virtual Reference Service*. Chicago: American Library Association.

DiGilio, John J., and Gayle Lynn-Nelson. 2004. "The Millennial Invasion: Are You Ready?" *Information Outlook* 8, no. 11 (November): 15–16, 18–20.

Gardner, Susan, and Susanna Eng. 2005. "What Students Want: Generation Y and the Changing Function of the Academic Library." *Portal* 5, no. 3 (July): 405–420.

Green, Jamie, Barbara Chivers, and Glen Mynott. 2000. "In the Librarian's Chair: An Analysis of Factors Which Influence the Motivation of Library Staff and Contribute to the Effective Delivery of Services." *Library Review* 49, no. 8: 380–386.

Horowitz, Lisa R., Patricia A. Flanagan, and Deborah L. Helman. 2005. "The Viability of Live Online Reference: An Assessment." *Portal: Libraries & the Academy* 5, no. 2 (April): 239–258.

Kern, M. Kathleen. 2004. "Chat It Up! Extending Reference Services to Assist Off-Campus Students." *Journal of Library Administration* 41, no. 1/2: 217–226.

Lancaster, Lynne C. 2003. "The Click and Clash of Generations." *Library Journal* 128, no. 17 (October 15): 36–39.

Lippincott, Joan. 2005. "Net Generation Students and Libraries." In *Educating the Net Generation*. Edited by Diana Oblinger and James L. Oblinger (pp 13.1–13.14). Boulder, CO: EDUCAUSE. Available: www.educause.edu/EducatingtheNet Generation/5989

Masters, Denise G. 1996. "Total Quality Management in Libraries." (ED396759) ERIC Database (January 2006). Available: www. eric.ed.gov

Stemper, James A., and John T. Butler. 2001. "Developing a Model to Provide Digital Reference Services." *Reference Services Review* 29, no. 3: 172–188.

Sweeney, Richard T. 2005. "Reinventing Library Buildings and Services for the Millennial Generation." *Library Administration & Management* 19, no. 4 (Fall): 165–175.

Waldman, David A. 1994. "Designing Performance Management Systems for Total Quality Implementation." *Journal of Organizational Change Management* 7, no. 2: 31–44.

Ward, Joyce, Dana Mervar, Matthew Loving, and Steve Kronen. 2003. "Going It Alone: Can a Small/Medium-Sized Library Manage Live Online Reference?" *Reference Librarian* 38, no. 79/80 (November): 311–322.

Part II

Branching Out

Adding Instant Messaging to an Established Virtual Reference Service: Asking "r u there?"

Pam Sessoms and Jean Ferguson

Overview
The Duke University libraries and the Davis Library at the University of North Carolina at Chapel Hill added IM to their mature VR offerings. Both chose Gaim, an open-source, multi-protocol IM client, available free online. The AOL IM client is supported by both libraries, and UNC's Davis Library also provides service for Yahoo and MSN.

With the introduction of IM, the universities developed:

- staffing models, with special attention given to shift change protocols
- training techniques, including those intended to address concerns held by staff who have not previously used IM

A statistical analysis shows the impact of IM on existing VR service.

Introduction and Background
Instant Messaging (IM) is extremely popular with the 18–27 year old age group, also known as Gen Y. IM reference service provides a unique opportunity for libraries to connect with this age group. Integrated features such as the IM 'Buddy List' encourage repeat sessions, as users can save the IM reference service as one of their 'Buddies.' The 'Buddy List' also is an easy way for users to see when the service is available, as an icon typically appears only when the service is on.

While most users find IM extremely easy to install and use, the software lacks the integrated back end of the commercial Virtual Reference (VR) packages. Individual logins for each staff member, statistics collection, and queuing are a few features currently absent from most IM clients. These differences can make providing an IM reference service daunting, especially if a library has come to rely on a commercial package.

Many libraries who currently offer VR services through a commercial provider, such as Tutor.com or QuestionPoint-24/7, are becoming interested in adding IM to their existing service as a method of reaching a wider audience. Concerns include implications for the commercial service, along with training and staffing issues.

The Lay of the Land

The University of North Carolina at Chapel Hill had 27,276 students enrolled in 2005. Of these, 61 percent were undergraduates, and the remaining 39 percent were graduate and professional school students (University of North Carolina at Chapel Hill, 2005). The Davis Library is the main research library on the UNC-CH campus. There is a separate undergraduate library that also has its own instant messaging service. Approximately 19 staff members and a handful of library science graduate students staff the virtual reference service at the Davis Library. Their hours are from 9 a.m. to 9:45 p.m., Mondays through Thursdays, with reduced hours on Fridays and Sundays. The commercial virtual reference service is also staffed through a three-school local consortium from 9 p.m. to midnight, Sundays through Thursdays.

Duke University enrolled 12,085 students. Of these, 50 percent were undergraduates, and the other 50 percent were graduate and professional school students (Duke University, 2007). The Perkins Library is the main research library on the Duke campus. The Divinity School Library has its own separate instant messaging service. Twenty-two librarians and four graduate students share the staffing of the overall virtual reference service. Hours are from 11a.m. to midnight, Mondays through Thursdays, with reduced hours on Fridays, Saturdays, and Sundays. Duke's commercial virtual reference service is staffed by the same three school consortium as UNC's from 9 p.m. to midnight, Sundays through Thursdays, while instant messaging is staffed in-house during these hours.

Why IM?

Both Duke and UNC-Chapel Hill chose to implement an instant messaging service based on the needs of their users. According to the Pew Internet and American Life report on instant messaging, 62 percent of 18–27 year olds currently use instant messaging. Of this group, 57 percent use IM more than e-mail (Shiu, 2004). Given that both schools have a large population of students within this age bracket, it was a natural choice to consider software with which the users were already familiar. The Undergraduate Library at UNC-Chapel Hill launched an extremely successful IM service, and UNC-Chapel Hill library science graduate students soon spread the word and enthusiasm for IM through Davis and Perkins while working in student jobs, internships, and, upon graduation, professional positions.

Commercial Virtual Reference vs. Instant Messaging

There are many advantages and disadvantages to using either the commercially available virtual reference software or instant messaging. Commercial VR software, for example, allows one to check if the next librarian staffing the service has signed in. It also keeps statistics through its backend and generates reports. Most of the VR software available today does not require any type of software download on the librarian side, and sometimes none on the user's side. Audio alerting will occur through a bell or other type of sound until the session is picked up by a librarian. The single public identity for multiple librarians also is transparent to the user. The final benefit of the commercial VR software is that users do not need to register with a vendor in order to ask a question.

Instant messaging has the benefit of having an installed user base. This is especially true of the America Online AIM protocol, which commands 43 percent of university Internet users (Shiu, 2004). The buddy list, where a user can save the screen names of others with whom they instant message frequently, encourages use as the IM name appears when the service is available. Also, as the instant messaging service was originally used for informal chatting with friends and colleagues, it is perceived as friendly and informal. Many instant messengers use all lower case letters, abbreviations, and smiley faces or other emoticons.

Some of the disadvantages of commercial virtual reference software include its relative instability, especially when attempting to use interactive co-browsing. Generally, the software is perceived as less intuitive to users who aren't already familiar with it. The librarian-side configuration also can be difficult, depending on the platform chosen.

Shift changes are unclear when using instant messaging. Statistics are kept manually and can be very time-consuming to collect. Configuring the setup to automatically use the same preferences for all staff, as well as automatically save the transcripts for statistics collection, is not only time-consuming, depending on the number of librarians on the service, but also can be difficult depending on how systems are setup within the library. Some librarians also see instant messaging as unprofessional due to the emoticons and informal language. The default alert that a patron is waiting is a single sound but can be changed by the administrator. Both Duke and UNC-Chapel Hill also found that more spam is received through instant messaging than through the commercial virtual reference software. The final disadvantage is that patrons must register with a commercial entity, such as America Online, to use this service.

Statistics

The following two charts show the number of sessions held with the commercial virtual reference software per month at UNC-Chapel Hill (Figure 3-1) and Duke (Figure 3-2).

The darker line in Figures 3-3 and 3-4 below shows the number of sessions per month for virtual reference. The lighter line shows the number of instant messaging sessions for the same period. UNC-Chapel Hill saw fairly equal traffic with both the commercial virtual reference and instant messaging until the Fall, when instant messaging rose considerably. Duke experienced higher instant messaging traffic from the launch of the service and a continued rise in the number of sessions over time.

Figure 3-1: Virtual Reference Traffic at UNC-Chapel Hill for the Commercial Virtual Reference Software

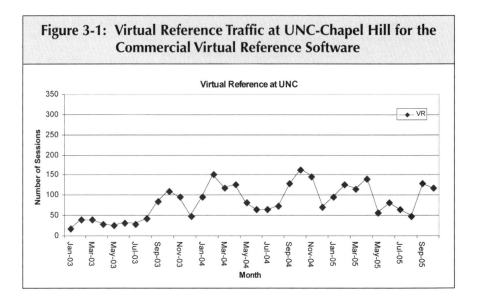

Figure 3-2: Virtual Reference Traffic at Duke for the Commercial Virtual Reference Software

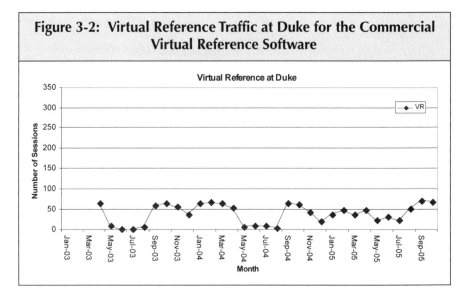

As shown in Figures 3-5 and 3-6, the darker line represents virtual reference traffic and the lighter line shows us the number of instant messaging sessions per month. The line designated throughout by triangles is the sum of both virtual reference and instant messaging traffic at both UNC-Chapel Hill and Duke. As you can see, through adding instant messaging to the overall chat service, both schools generally maintained their commercial virtual reference traffic, saw a spike in traffic over time with instant messaging, and more

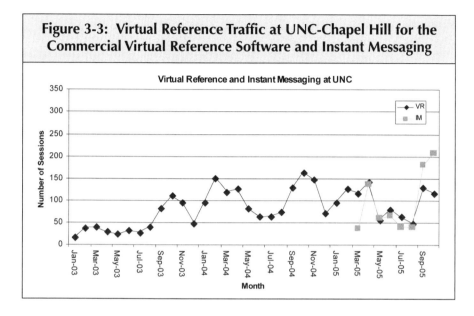

Figure 3-3: Virtual Reference Traffic at UNC-Chapel Hill for the Commercial Virtual Reference Software and Instant Messaging

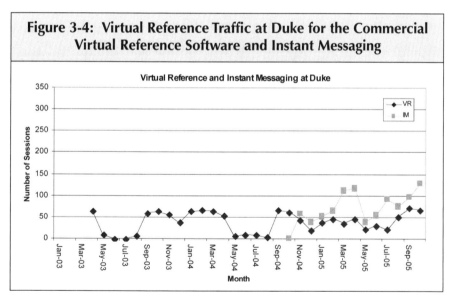

Figure 3-4: Virtual Reference Traffic at Duke for the Commercial Virtual Reference Software and Instant Messaging

than doubled their total number of sessions. The top line shows the combined VR and IM traffic

Staffing Models

Staffing an instant messaging service is similar to staffing the reference desk. There are several models from which to choose. Generally, the two obvious

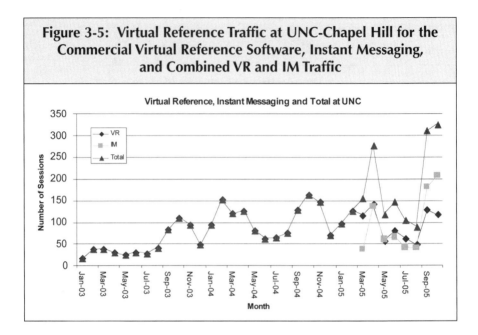

Figure 3-5: Virtual Reference Traffic at UNC-Chapel Hill for the Commercial Virtual Reference Software, Instant Messaging, and Combined VR and IM Traffic

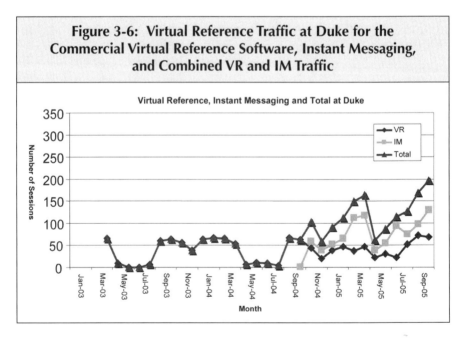

Figure 3-6: Virtual Reference Traffic at Duke for the Commercial Virtual Reference Software, Instant Messaging, and Combined VR and IM Traffic

choices are either staffing the service from the Reference desk or from the individual desks of the librarians. UNC-Chapel Hill has chosen a unique model by placing the computer hosting the instant messaging software in the Reference offices that are located directly behind the desk (Figure 3-7). A speaker is placed near the door so that librarians can hear the alert when a new patron is waiting. The benefit to this system is that no shift change procedure is required as chat is essentially staffed by the librarians at the desk. To create a repetitive alert system, UNC-Chapel Hill altered a sound file to have it repeat after 20 seconds in case it was not heard the first time. Unfortunately, with Gaim, the multiprotocol software which both UNC-Chapel Hill and Duke are using, the sound file will only play once and not repeat until picked up, as is the case with the commercial virtual reference software.

Duke has chosen a hybrid staffing model that varies depending on the time of day and academic calendar. During the day, which generally has the highest traffic for instant messaging as well as for the Reference desk, librarians staff the service from their own computers. From 6 p.m. to midnight, during the week, the service is staffed from the Reference desk. In the summer months, during academic breaks, and when many librarians are away from the library for an event, the service is also staffed from the Reference desk due to reduced instant messaging and desk traffic.

One disadvantage to this hybrid model is that the computers of all the librarians staffing the service, as well as those at the Reference desk, must be

Figure 3-7: The Virtual Reference Computers behind the Desk at UNC

configured to automatically save transcripts of the sessions for statistics. Shift changes when staffing at the librarians desk also can be confusing, as an instant message conversation may be in progress when a new librarian signs on. Instant messaging does not provide any method to indicate if this is a new message or ongoing message. Patrons can get confused, as well, if two librarians signed on to the same user name respond, because the patron will see both responses but neither librarian can see what the other librarian has typed. AOL instant messaging also provides a screen showing you how many other users are signed on to the same screen name at the same time when you sign on (Figure 3-8). It allows you to type "1" to disconnect all the other users. As Duke would prefer that only one librarian be signed on to a screen name at any time to prevent user confusion, sometimes one librarian disconnects a second inadvertently in mid-conversation.

Marketing

As with any public service, it is important to let the users know of its existence. Duke and UNC-Chapel Hill employed many traditional and non-traditional

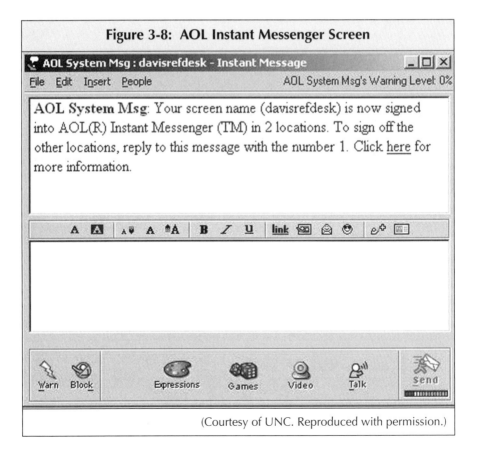

Figure 3-8: AOL Instant Messenger Screen

(Courtesy of UNC. Reproduced with permission.)

methods of getting the word out. The first step for both schools was marketing internally so that librarians would mention the service in library instruction courses, at the Reference and Circulation desk, and at meetings with faculty and other campus groups. A Web page described each school's service and was linked from the library home page through the AskA Librarian information.

Electronic marketing included changing the wallpaper on all of the public terminals in the library to advertise the instant messaging service, as well as creating screen savers to do the same. Duke also created an icon on the desktop of the public computers that, when double-clicked, opened the Web page describing the instant messaging service and provided links to it. UNC-Chapel Hill and Duke also had e-mail signatures from their Reference desk account, which listed their instant messaging screen name as one of the available resources.

Lower tech methods have included the creation of fliers that were posted in public spaces around campus, such as bus stops, the student center, the dining hall, and other well-trafficked locations. UNC-Chapel Hill created tear-off tabs on their flier with the instant message screen names. The school additionally created a small 'My Name Is' sticker that listed their screen name (Figure 3-9). With laptops being a requirement, students often stick these stickers right on their laptops for easy access. Duke created a business card

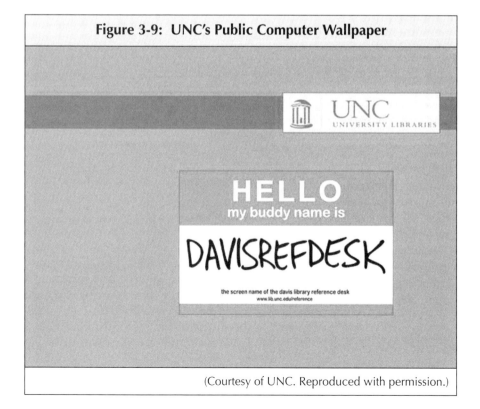

Figure 3-9: UNC's Public Computer Wallpaper

(Courtesy of UNC. Reproduced with permission.)

Figure 3-10: Duke's Public Computer Wallpaper

(Courtesy of Duke University. Reproduced with permission.)

listing their instant message name which they handed out at the Reference Desk and in library instruction (Figure 3-10).

The wallpaper shown in Figure 3-10 appeared in many libraries across campus. The Ask a Librarian services were advertised including the instant message screen name. Icons on the left side linked to the Ask a Librarian Service and to instant messaging.

Training

UNC had all librarians sign up for individual instant message accounts. They practiced internally with each other to become comfortable with the software and instant messaging culture. The virtual reference coordinator then held a formal workshop to go through the software use, as well as procedures. Duke's virtual reference coordinator spent time individually with each librarian while installing and configuring the software for the service, then held a group workshop. Both schools found that the software for instant messaging was much more intuitive and easier for librarians to use than the commercial virtual reference package. It was helpful to provide librarians with lists of acronyms to allay staff anxiety about chat lingo.

Just-in-Time Training

As with any new service, the initial training was a good foundation but smaller just-in-time training sessions were held to make librarians aware of new concepts. Examples of this kind of session were how to respond to a rash of spam or viruses over instant messaging; how to deal with abusive, repetitive, or silly patrons; and how to handle bots that ask circular questions. Initially, librarians at Duke had difficulty taking some of the screen names seriously but have found over time that it's more important to assess the question than the screen name.

Teaching the culture of instant messaging is often cause for short training sessions during regularly scheduled meetings. Instant messengers often use very informal grammar, lowercase letters, and little or no punctuation. It is important for librarians, as they do on the commercial virtual reference software, to be explicit in their actions and to type everything that they are doing so that the user is aware that they haven't been forgotten. Sending several short phrases or sentences as opposed to a single paragraph is one method for ensuring this.

Back End

Virtual reference coordinators that already manage a commercial virtual reference system will probably find IM's lack of an integrated back end management system a bit daunting at first. However, there are a number of tricks and configuration changes that can be made to provide a number of useful managerial functions within an IM service. Using the Gaim software, UNC-Chapel Hill has set up centralized locations for Gaim's configuration files and automatic logging. The centralized configuration makes setup on multiple librarian computers much easier, while automatic logging allows library staff to read transcripts for quality control, training, patron follow-up, and statistics-gathering purposes.

Gaim's centralized settings rely on creating a system environment variable for the desired location of Gaim configuration files. This location can be a network drive in order to facilitate access from multiple computers on a network. The environment variable can be set manually, or systems staff may find it more convenient to set it automatically via a registry edit called a system login script. To set the variable manually, the following steps should be followed:

1. Right-click on 'My Computer' and select 'Properties.'
2. Select the 'Advanced' tab.
3. Select the 'Environment Variables' button.
4. Select the 'New' button in 'System Variables.'
5. Set the variable name GAIMHOME to the desired location (for instance, g:\gaimlogs).
6. Select OK three times to get out of the 'Systems Properties' dialog.

If Gaim has already been installed locally, the configuration files can be copied from their current location to the network location. The default location is: c:\documents and settings\username\ application data\.gaim

Within Gaim, logging must be enabled. This is done by starting Gaim and then selecting Tools → Preferences → Logging. "Log all instant messages" and "Log all chats" should both be enabled. UNC-Chapel Hill is using the plain text format for its logs since they are easy to read, open quickly, and can be parsed using scripting languages such as Perl. The logs will be saved in a consistent, tree-like structure in the following manner (assuming g:\gaimlogs is the centralized directory): G:\gaimlogs\.gaim\logs\ protocol name\library buddy name\patron buddy name\date. timestarted.txt

So, an AIM chat between davisrefdesk and unc-gal on December 11, 2005, at 12:33 p.m. would be: G:\gaimlogs\.gaim\logs\ AIM\davisrefdesk\unc-gal\2005-12-11.123300.txt

Staff members can be trained to navigate quickly to the most recent chats by using their standard My Computer browsing techniques and sorting by date. Logs open easily in a text editor such as Notepad, and each line is given a timestamp so it is possible to calculate the chat's duration.

There are a few caveats of which staff members need to be made aware when enabling centralized logging and other shared configuration settings. First, each computer that has the GAIMHOME environment variable set and logging enabled will log all chats done through Gaim. This means that if someone is using Gaim for their own personal IM on one of these computers, their private chats will be logged. UNC-Chapel Hill has emphasized this fact in training and encourages staff members to use a native IM client or Trillian for personal IM rather than Gaim. Next, UNC-Chapel Hill has found it convenient to have Gaim automatically log in all accounts when Gaim starts in order to eliminate staff confusion about signing in multiple protocols (AIM, Yahoo!, MSN). This means that staff working on computers with a Gaim icon should not start Gaim at all unless they are signing in the public IM service, since simply starting the program will login davisrefdesk, the public IM identity, on that computer.

Script
One of the most beloved features of commercial VR packages is the reporting system. These systems allow easy collection of usage statistics. IM packages are generally lacking this feature. UNC-Chapel Hill is developing a Perl script that will parse Gaim logs and provide simple usage statistics (Figure 3-11).

This script is still under development, but, once it is usable, it will be shared freely with other libraries.

Future
There are exciting future directions for IM services in all areas. Marketing remains a key ingredient in a successful program, and social networking strategies seem to be a natural fit for such social software. A library identity in Facebook, for instance, might be a good way for college and university libraries to reach their students. Another idea is marketing IM service to students in locations where they might benefit from virtual service. For instance, at Duke University, many students spend days at a time camping in a "tent

Figure 3-11: A Summary Report from the Script for October 2005

10 2005:

    Total chats   : 214
    Longest: 01   :19:16
    Average: 00 :08:56
    Median: 00   :05:47

        Total chats (aim): 184
        Shortest   : 00:00:00
        Longest   : 01:19:16
        Average   : 00:08:33
        Median   : 00:05:40

        Total chats (yahoo): 24
        Shortest   : 00:00:00
        Longest   : 00:56:13
        Average   : 00:11:32
        Median   : 00:06:07

        Total chats (msn): 6
        Shortest   : 00:01:59
        Longest   : 00:21:13
        Average   : 00:10:22
        Median   : 00:09:30

city" for basketball tickets, and they are not likely to leave this area in order to visit the library in person. Fliers or other advertising placed in the vicinity might be a good way to let them know that they can take advantage of the library IM services through the wireless campus network. Signs on campus and town busses are another interesting idea.

In the technical arena, there are many opportunities. IM additions onto existing commercial VR packages would be wonderful and would allow many libraries to integrate their services or to expand into IM more easily. Standardized scripts for statistics gathering and report generation would be wonderful. A queuing system that would allow multiple librarians to be signed into IM simultaneously and receive incoming IMs directed to a single screen name is another critical need. This is the main "missing link" that, if available, would allow large cooperative IM efforts to begin; imagine a state-wide IM service with a single librarian identity, with multiple librarians simultaneously helping multiple patrons, all seamlessly.

References

Duke University. Office of News & Communications. 2007. "Duke at a Glance" Durham, NC: Duke University. Available: www.duke news.duke.edu/resources/quickfacts.html#students

Shiu, Eulynn. "How Americans Use Instant Messaging." Washington, DC: Pew Internet & American Life Project. (September 2004) Available: www.pewinternet.org/PPF/r/133/report_display.asp

University of North Carolina at Chapel Hill: Finance. "Student Head Count and FTE Enrollment. Educational Level and Residency." Chapel Hill, NC: University of North Carolina at Chapel Hill (November 2005) Available: www.unc.edu/finance/data/ST-Headcount-FTE.pdf

Chapter 4

Responding to Triage Taxonomy: Answering Virtual Medical Questions

Catherine Arnott Smith

Overview
Popular interest in medical information is at an all-time high; eight out of ten Internet users—95 million Americans—have searched for health information. The potential virtual reference audience for health-related questions grows every day. Unfortunately, due to liability concerns, the typical virtual reference service declines to answer medical questions, defining them as "outside the scope of the service."

An automated process that distinguished resource questions—"Where can I find a support group for cancer patients?"—from diagnosis questions—"Do I have cancer?"—could expand the scope and usefulness of virtual reference services in this area of high need. Such a process would require a taxonomy for medical questions.

The author discusses why consumer health questions pose particular challenges to virtual reference services in all kinds of information settings and introduces the Triage Taxonomy as a potential solution.

Introduction and Background
There is nothing new about consumer interest in health information in the United States. Although the 1970s is generally credited as the historical birth of consumer health, the provision and production of health information intended expressly for the public is a process as old as the printing press (Greenberg, 1997), and formal collecting of health information for the lay reader in the United States has been documented since the nineteenth century. Patient education incorporating libraries and library resources began in 1905, when a Dr. Platt, of Boston, set up what later generations would call a bibliotherapy group for people with tuberculosis needing information and support (Rubin, 1983).

The first professionally oriented article for medical librarians to approach the subject of consumer health was published in 1921 in the *Bulletin of the Medical Library Association*. Since the Medical Library Association was founded by three librarians and three physicians, many early articles were speeches delivered by physicians at the MLA's annual meeting; Dr. J.W. Farlow's was typical of its kind. He said: "An ever-increasing number of the community is taking a larger and larger interest in medicine and health and wishes to get in touch with some of the helpful books on medical subjects. . . . We cannot help noticing a very lively interest on the part of the public in subjects which, not so very long ago, were supposed to be the monopoly of the medical profession" (Farlow, 1921: 3).

In discussing the provision of this information to a hungry public, Farlow stated flatly that the public library cannot be expected to meet the demand, because medical subjects are out of the librarians' scope of expertise. While he commented that reference requests from the public received at his medical library were always "cheerfully answered," he went on to warn that this was because "The public library knows little, and consequently cares little, about medical books" (Farlow, 1921: 3).

Seventeen years later, similar opinions were expressed by a medical publisher named Williams (founder of Williams & Wilkins). Speaking at another MLA annual meeting in 1934, Williams called "health books" a very popular subject among the public, although "a few years ago" there was little on the market except home doctor books for farm families. However, Williams called some of these popular texts "not very authoritative," which posed a collection development problem for public libraries. In fact, the publisher questioned whether public libraries should be collecting this material at all: "Would not the public libraries be glad to be relieved of the responsibility from much of the misleading information now on the shelves, by turning over to local and medical libraries the work of supplying popular but authoritative books on medical and health subjects?" (Williams, 1934: 94).

The fears of these early writers appear to have mirrored the anxieties of public librarians of the day, even in the face of dramatically increasing consumer interest in consumer health.

The creation myths of the consumer health movement generally ascribe it to a mix of social, political, and economic forces exerting pressure in the 1970s, including women's rights and consumer empowerment. A number of contemporary writers were careful to note, however, that it was the amplitude of demand for consumer health information that had changed; it was the amount and the kind of information available that had increased so notably since the 1960s. Consumer health thus became every librarian's problem.

Web-Based Consumer Health Information Seeking

The changes in mass communication that took place because of the World Wide Web accentuated an interest in health information among the general public that had been there for years.

The long-running survey research conducted by the Pew Internet & American Life Project (www.pewinternet.org) published its first health-specific report, "The Online Health Care Revolution: How the Web Helps Americans Take Better Care of Themselves in 2000" (Fox and Rainie, 2000). Although market researchers had been tracking health information seeking online for several years, the Pew Report was significant for being the first research conducted by a nonprofit entity to yield authoritative data about Internet health information-seeking behavior. A second report investigating expectations of Internet users, and including "health" as one of its focus areas, was published in December 2002: "Counting on the Internet" (Horrigan and Rainie, 2002). A third study, "Health Information Online," followed up the 2002 report and revealed general trends in health information-seeking (Fox, 2005).

One contribution of the Pew surveys has been the description of Internet users likely to be looking for health information online. Fox's second report (2005) found the most likely cyber-information seekers were women, Internet users under 65, college graduates, people with extensive online experience, and people with broadband connections.

The Pew study in 2002 found that eight out of 10 Internet users had looked for health information online, a statistic unchanged in 2005. The typical health information seeker in 2005 was looking for information about specific doctors and hospitals; experimental treatments, including alternative medicine; health insurance; medicines; fitness; and nutrition. These were categories that saw statistically significant differences in 2005, compared to the earlier study. However, the most popular health topic remained the same: "a specific disease or medical problem" (Horrigan and Rainie, 2002).

Ethical Dimensions of Consumer Health Information Practice

Medical questions are problematic for all librarians and information professionals in all settings. Sandra Wood (1991: 244) noted that, although the core ethical concerns are the same in the health domain as they are outside it— "Access to information, quality of service, confidentiality, neutrality, intellectual freedom"—health information does present health-specific challenges.

First, the technical language in which the information is available presents difficulties for patrons, and librarians often find themselves translating as well as informing. In Vanderbilt University Medical Center's medical library's PICS project, for example, librarians prepare customized information packets translated to 'consumer-ese,' when necessary, to fill information prescriptions written by physicians (Williams et al., 2001). Second, the quality necessary in the health information domain is of paramount importance because information that is wrong or old can be actively dangerous.

In addition, the provision of health information can impose a stressful situation on the provider. Several authors contributing to a special issue of the reference journal RQ point out that stress occurs because medical questions tend to be personal (Dewdney et al., 1991); library staff can be perceived, inaccurately, as a free counseling service (Alloway and Salisbury, 1983); and librarians who sincerely wish to help will experience a conflict between service to their "client" and to others waiting in line. Finally, the information being provided can itself be upsetting to people on either side of the reference desk, because medical information can carry very, very bad news. For this reason, medical questions have been compared to legal questions; both types "tend to arise from highly personal problems that the user may not wish to disclose to the librarian, or, as William A. Katz points out, which the librarian may not wish to hear" (Dewdney et al., 1991: 193).

From this arises the well-documented librarian resistance to medical questions. The same William A. Katz quoted by Dewdney stated in the very first edition of his classic reference services textbook, *Introduction to Reference Work* (1982: 240), that

> At one time, reference librarians hesitated to answer any type of medical question.... A few librarians still believe medical reference questions should not be answered, or only in a noncommittal way, such as sending the patron to the card catalog... because the librarian fears possible complications.

This fear of "possible complications" has been called "the golden rule of medical reference. At no point does the librarian interpret or evaluate the information retrieved" (Katz, 1982: 240). This directive is only alluded to in the *RUSA Guidelines for Medical Information Service Responses*, published in their second edition (Reference and User Services Association, 2001). These Guidelines state explicitly that "a library's information services staff must have the knowledge and preparation appropriate to meet the routine legal, medical, or business information needs of their clientele" (sec. 1.0.1) while hedging their bets with sec. 1.0.3: "Libraries should develop written disclaimers stating a policy on providing specialized information service denoting variations in types and levels of service. The level of assistance and interpretation provided to users should reflect differing degrees of subject expertise between specialists and non-specialists."

These ethical dilemmas and sensitivities are part of the inheritance of virtual reference services. Despite the common-sense appeal of providing medical reference in a public library setting, public libraries always have experienced a certain tension around medical questions. On the one hand, they have recognized a public crying out for medical information and have the accurate perception that a different and a more specialized training is required for the average generalist to handle it. This tension is apparent in the training future librarians receive in LIS schools and programs, where medical information has traditionally been seen as the province of future medical librarians taking special courses in medical reference or medical searching. These specialists attend conferences held by specialized associations such as the Medical Library Association (the oldest specialist library association in the country); they may also have special undergraduate or graduate backgrounds, for example, biology degrees or health paraprofessional experience. In addition, medical librarians who work in medical libraries, precisely because they are specialized, have the luxury of complete focus on the one subject area of "health"—a large subject area, to be sure, but still enabling focus. Public librarians, conversely, have other constituencies to serve besides consumers seeking health information. These constituencies affect their funding, the training they are able to receive in school and post-MLS, and finally the information resources that are acquired and maintained by their public libraries. The resources available to answer consumer health questions in public library settings will inevitably reflect and reinforce differences from medical libraries in librarians' background, expertise, and service priorities. The dilemma of the twenty-first century librarian, then, is that consumer health information practice—no matter where it is located—requires a medical librarian's knowledge of information resources, particularly information retrieval, and a public librarian's customer service skills.

Before the World Wide Web, many public libraries could sidestep these differences by referring patrons to medical libraries. The Web, however, has completely changed the equation. Because the Web exposes much more medical information to a much wider audience, "What was an occasional question thirty years ago has become a torrent of increasingly specific requests" (Gillaspy, 2000: 5).

Medical Questions and Virtual Reference

It is no surprise, then, that virtual reference services exhibit the professional tensions around medical information that began in physical reference settings. In fact, among the virtual reference services that explicitly exclude certain question types, all of them exclude medical questions.

A common example of this restriction is found in the privacy policy at the Internet Public Library (2005): "Please note that some questions submitted to the IPL may be rejected because they are out of scope (medical, legal) or above the daily quota (no volunteer staff available)."

A small sample is presented by the list of AskA services listed at the Information Institute's VRD Web site in the "Health" category (VRD, 2005). Thirteen AskA services are listed, of which 12 are functioning as of this writing. Figure 4-1 one shows the proportion of these AskA services that have stated policies about medical questions.

Development of the Triage Taxonomy

"Triage" is a medical term deriving from the French trier, "to sort" (Simpson and Weiner, 1989) and was originally coined in the eighteenth century to mean "assortment according to quality." Adapted to medical use and appearing in medical context as early as 1930, it refers to the procedure of distinguishing between patients with urgent need of care and those who can wait. "Triage" was chosen as a name for this question taxonomy because the taxonomy itself is designed to bridge the worlds of clinical medicine and consumer health information practice.

This taxonomy was developed to assist with analysis of data from the Ten Thousand Questions project, the first winner of the Donald A. B. Lindberg

Figure 4-1: AskA Services and Policies

AskA Service	URL	Policy?	Language
About College	www.aboutcollege. com/	None stated	
Ask NSDL	ask.nsdl.org/services/ asknsdl/AskNSDL_ policies.aspx	Yes	"Experts will not be expected to provide answers to questions requiring an opinion on any moral, ethical, legal, medical or otherwise controversial topics."
Ask EPA	http://epa-kids.custhelp. com	None stated	
Food Timeline	www.foodtimeline.org/ index.html	None stated	
Ask Jack	http://www.naysi. com/ask_jack/ask_ jack.htm	None stated	
Kentucky Center for School Safety	www.kysafeschools. org/contact/	None stated	
Sex, etc.	www.sexetc.org/page / glossary/	Yes	"The information contained within the Sex, Etc. Web site does not constitute medical, legal or other professional advice."
Children with Diabetes	www.childrenwith diabetes. com/index_ cwd.htm	Yes	"The opinions expressed are for general information only and should not be construed as medical advice or diagnosis, nor as advice about treatment of any specific medical condition."
Go Ask Alice!	www.goaskalice. columbia.edu	Yes	"Go Ask Alice! provides health information and should not be considered specific medical advice, a diagnosis, treatment, or a second opinion for health conditions."

(Cont'd.)

Figure 4-1: AskA Services and Policies (Continued)

AskA Service	URL	Policy?	Language
NetWellness	www.netwellness.org/	Yes	"Please note: only your personal physician or other health professional you consult can best advise you on matters of your health based on your medical history, your family medical history, your medication history, and how information from any of these databases may apply to you."
Neuroscientist Network	http://faculty.washington.edu/chudler/questions.html	Yes	"NOTE: the Neuroscientist Network will not diagnose your illness or give you medical or legal advice."
Ask a Parenting Expert	http://life.family education.com/parenting/parenting-problem-solving/39558.html?detoured=1	Yes	"... Any information received from this Advice Area is not intended to diagnose, treat, or cure. This site is for information purposes only. The information on this Advice Area is not intended to replace proper medical care."

Research Fellowship, a new research award given by the Medical Library Association. For this project, 10,000 posts were harvested from Web-based bulletin boards that focus on health. These bulletin boards are all English-language, no-cost and/or no registration required, online communities. It should be noted that "English-language" does not equate to "American," despite the heavy U.S. presence on the Web generally. One bulletin board is sponsored by an English broadcasting company, and another is sponsored by an Indian organization.

All were included in subject directories provided by seven major search engines (AltaVista, AOL Search, Google, LookSmart, Netscape, Open Directory, and Yahoo!) and identified because they were classed under Health Advice and synonymous categories.

This methodology yielded a gross total of 514 bulletin boards. One hundred and thirty-eight (27 percent) were duplicates, listings included in more than one subject directory. This left a net total of 376 bulletin boards. Of those 376, only 48 (13 percent) met the selection criteria (English-language, free and/or no registration required, and functioning). One further selection criterion: Postings from participants in these online bulletin boards could not show signs of having been edited by Web site owners, since it was felt that this would invalidate conclusions about "consumer" terminology and expression of information needs.

From this final list of 48, boards were selected using a "popularity" metric. "Popularity" was operationalized through the Google Link Popularity Analysis Tool; bulletin boards were ranked in descending order according to the number of Web sites linking to them (links ranged from 12,900 to 15,100). This metric was chosen to ensure that the bulletin boards harvested for text were boards that were considerably exposed on the Web and thus likely to be representative of well-trafficked Web communities and the language of those communities. The 48 sites with which analysis began dropped to 25 over the course of data collection, since some of the 48 proved to be extremely low-traffic (15 or fewer posts in a month) and yielded very little data for analysis.

The focus of these bulletin boards ranges from general parenting issues (childhood illness, learning disabilities, etc.) through specific diagnoses, both adult and pediatric, to fitness and wellness, including sexual health. Nonmedical subtopics on these boards (for example, "Career and Work Issues") were not collected.

Figure 4-2 presents some exemplar posts from the large collection. Most posts contain more than one question and present the reference librarian in every library setting—including the virtual reference desk—with a range of challenges, including ethical challenges. All spellings and phrasings are verbatim.

Why worry about a taxonomy? Not only does a classification of questions help us understand consumers' information needs, and ideally help us *meet* those needs by providing the resources they want, but it also could inform development of a Web-based assist, a navigation aid that would point consumers toward the most specific resources for their answers.

The way to do this is to find out what taxonomies exist for the content of interest, test those existing taxonomies for goodness of fit, and in the process create an enhanced taxonomy to be used by others. The taxonomy-building process improves the researcher's understanding of the data. The closeness of fit between data and the knowledge structure into which the data fits is what makes taxonomies useful.

To ensure good coverage of the range of questions expressed by consumers, it is necessary to leave the box of Library Literature to discover what taxonomies exist already, so as to exploit those structures and refine them to suit the new needs.

The literature on information seeking by physicians is extensive, particularly in consideration of the information resources they need. However, typical studies in clinical information seeking have been focused on the use of bibliographic resources. As Forsythe et al. (1992) mentions, MEDLINE assumes that the appropriate response to a query is a set of bibliographic citations to the medical literature. Thus, the taxonomies appearing in literature arise from questions relating directly to the medical literature and thus presume a clinical specialist of some kind is asking the question. The library patron or health care consumer is not generally the focus of the investigation.

Figure 4-2: Sample Consumer Health Posts and Questions

* I would like you to answer the following questions for me on tuberculosis . . . 1. What is it? 2. How do you get it? 3. On average how many people get it? 4. Is it hereditary? 5. Are there treatments? 6. Can it kill you? 7. Is it contagious? 8. Is it cureable? 9. When was it first discovered? 10. If I have this where should I go to be tested or treated? 11. What kind of treatment would I recive? 12. What kind of tests would I receive? 13. Which organ or organ system does it affect? ***** PLEASE ANSWER MY QUESTIONS & E-MAIL ME*****

*Is leukimia contageous? Do many people die from it ?

Hello, I am writing a novel in which one character tries to kill himself using a hypo filled with heroine. I need to know how much heroine it would take to cause death in an average-sized male, what would likely be in the syringe (typically . . . 100% heroine?), and what the fluid would look like. Thank you in advance for your service.

*Hi I am a 9th grader and i want to know more how to become a pediatrician but i want to work in the nursey with all the newborns is there a specific name for that? Another thing i would like to know is how long do you have to been in school for that specific job like working in the nusery?

Could you please tell me if there is a way for me to find out what my stepchildrens blood type is without asking their mother. Also I would like to find out what their mothers blood type is. You see I don't beleive the father is who she claims. I would like to know the truth, if these are my husbands children or not.

*Why is it that seeing or hearing someone else yawn, or even THINKING about yawning, prompts a yawn? What is the physiological function of a yawn? Thanks for your help. This unanswered question has been bugging me for years.

*I'd like advice on possible causes as well as what type of physician would be best suited to treat my condition. I'm female, about 5'7', 38 years old, 210 pounds. I'm a successful software engineer, highly assertive, very social, and enjoy leading and organizing projects. Other general health problems and conditions that may or may not be related: a inability to lose weight in spite of excercising 35–40 minutes 4–5 times a week and sensible diet, extremely oily skin, acne, scaly skin growths on my scalp and ears, a tendency towards 'spotting' up a week before my period, and being able to express a few drops of milky-liquid from my breast in spite of the fact that haven't nursed a baby since December 1989. I also had gallstones and thus my gall-bladder removed in 1990.

Who exactly invented acupuncture. When was acupuncture invented? How was acupuncture invented? Was acupuncture invented by accident and carried on as a Chinese invention or was acupuncture planned to be an invention?

For question taxonomies, researchers in the social sciences have relied heavily on the work of Graesser, which is grounded in artificial intelligence and discourse processing. Graesser's original taxonomy of questions (1994) has been recycled numerous times to classify questions from physical to virtual reference services. Both Graesser's taxonomy and questions were, however, developed in the nonmedical realm. Exhaustive literature searching has narrowed the field to four taxonomical candidates. These taxonomies, together with examples of questions that might appear in these categories, are listed in Figures 4-3, 4-4, 4-5, and 4-6. Taxonomies are from the published literature as cited; examples were created by the author.

The oldest taxonomy (Roter, 1984), was created for a study of verbal patient-physician communication and derived from audiotaped clinic visits. Although this is a relatively old study, Marilyn White, at University of Maryland, who has done much work on questions, used Roter's taxonomy from 1984 to apply to consumer health questions on an electronic listserv (White, 2000).

Graesser's taxonomy was discussed above. It is a multipurpose taxonomy developed to classify question types and has been retrofitted to serve numerous domains.

D'Alessandro and her colleagues are physicians who developed the Virtual Hospital site at the University of Iowa (www.vrd.org), one of the very first consumer health sites on the Web. This taxonomy was developed to sort e-mail questions for redirection to the appropriate physician.

Bhavnani et al.'s (2002) taxonomy categorizes questions that patients might have about dermatology-related issues. The purpose is to use knowledge about likely Web-based questions to develop a more effective portal for consumer searching.

The author took 100 random postings from a large collection of consumer questions and coded every question in this dataset using each of the four schemes: Roter's for patient questions, Graesser's for general questions, D'Alessandro's for e-mail questions, and Bhavnani's for dermatology. Although no single taxonomy was able to completely code every question, some were better than others. It was found that Bhavnani's taxonomy, intended to help in structuring very specific clinical questions about a very specific diagnosis, was unable to categorize non-dermatology questions easily. Graesser's, conversely, was so general that it would be useful only with extensive modification.

D'Alessandro's Virtual Hospital taxonomy and Roter's patient-questions taxonomy were much more useful. Because D'Alessandro's taxonomy was intended to answer the Virtual Hospital's questions about "What are our users asking for?" and because the data from that taxonomy was intended to inform clinicians about what clinical content to develop, this taxonomy was too heavy on clinical specialty and too light on consumer characteristics. Roter's was the opposite: Intended to categorize what consumers (patients, anyway) were actually saying in communication with a physician. A combination of the two taxonomies seemed to work best. Using this hybrid taxonomy allows us to grapple with the data and really understand what kinds of questions are really being asked by consumers in these online forums.

The final Triage Taxonomy combines aspects of Roter's and D'Alessandro's. The author has changed the name of Roter's "Health" to "Wellness" to reflect the more contemporary conception of what Roter meant (in the

Figure 4-3: Roter's Taxonomy

Category	Definition	Example
Nonmedical	Any question not specifically related to the disease	How do I get to your hospital from my house?
Diagnosis	All aspects of diagnosis, including examination, differential. Includes symptoms.	I have a cough and a cold and red spots on my chest. What have I got?
Diet	Discussion of food as related to the disease	Is fish oil any good to prevent heart disease?
Epidemiology	Incidence, prevalence, spread of disease, morbidity, and mortality	Is cancer contagious?
Etiology	The signs and study of the causes of disease and their modes of expression	Why do my kids both have asthma?
Health	Discussion of effects of smoking, alcohol use, and physical activity	Will drinking heavily affect your liver?
Medication	Use of drugs to allay symptoms	What is the best nonsteroidal anti-inflammatory drugs (NSAIDs) for arthritis relief?
Prevention	Increasing human or animal resistance against the disease; for example, by immunization; for control or transmission agents for prevention and control of environmental hazards, or for prevention and control of social factors related to disease. Includes preventive measures for individual cases.	Should my son be getting that new meningitis booster next year? He's 10.
Prognosis	Forecast of the probable course, or outcome of a disease, or both	Is my wife's broken leg going to be better soon?
Treatment	Discussion of other types of treatment besides medications and diet or multiple types of treatment.	What is the best treatment for a woman diagnosed with breast cancer?

(Based on information from "Patient Question Asking and Answering," published in the 1984 issue of *Health Psychology*.)

Figure 4-4: Graesser's Taxonomy

Category	Subcategory	Definition	Example
Short Answer			
	Verification	Is a fact true? Did an event occur?	Does vaccination cause disease?
	Disjunctive	Is X or Y the case? Is W, Y, or Z the case?	My kid has red spots all over her. Is that the measles or chicken pox?
	Concept completion	Who? What? What is the referent of a noun argument slot?	What is the name of the federal agency that sponsors disease research?
	Feature specification	What qualitative attributes does entity X have?	What are the first symptoms of ovarian cancer?
	Quantification	What is the value of a quantitative variable? How many?	How many colds does the average mother of a new-born get in the first year?
Long Answer			
	Definition	What does X mean?	What is "parakeet handler's disease?"
	Example	What is an example label or instance of the category?	What is one kind of repetitive stress injury?
	Comparison	How is X similar to Y? How is X different from Y?	Is it better for a kid to get chicken pox when they're a toddler or when they're older?
	Interpretation	What concept or claim can be inferred from a static or active pattern of data?	Men in our family all live to be in their nineties, and we've been farmers for six generations. Is this related?
	Causal antecedent	What state of event causally led to an event or state?	How did my husband get his liver disease?
			(Cont'd.)

		Figure 4-4: Graesser's Taxonomy *(Continued)*	
Category	Subcategory	Definition	Example
Long Answer *(Cont'd.)*			
	Causal consequence	What are the consequences of an event or state?	What happens to people who eat at McDonald's every day for a month?
	Goal orientation	What are the motives or goals behind an agent's action?	Why is the government coming out with so much information about the dangers of obesity?
	Instrumental	What instrument (single event or object) allows an agent to accomplish a goal?	What's the most effective diet for me?
	Procedural	What plan (procedure or set of acts) allows an agent to accomplish a goal?	What steps should I take to reduce my fat intake?
	Enablement	What object or resource allows an agent to perform an action?	What kind of dog is the best for companion animal therapy in a nursing home?
	Expectation	Why did some expected event not occur?	How come I didn't lose 50 pounds between Thanksgiving and New Year's?
	Judgmental	What value does the answer place on an idea or advice?	Is the American Academy of Pediatrics telling the truth about vaccinations?
Other			
	Assertion	The speaker makes a statement indicating he lacks knowledge or does not understand an idea.	Your website is telling me to go to MedlinePlus but I'm not sure what that is.

(Cont'd.)

Figure 4-4: Graesser's Taxonomy *(Continued)*

Category	Subcategory	Definition	Example
Other			
	Request	The speaker politely asks the listener to perform an action.	Please give me some information about Mad Cow Disease.
	Directive	The speaker wants the listener to perform an action and is spoken more forcefully than a request.	I really need information RIGHT NOW About Mad Cow Disease—I'm worried my sister has it.

(Based on information from "Question Asking and Answering," published in 1994 in *Handbook of Psycholinguists*.)

Figure 4-5: D'Alessandro's Taxonomy

Category	Subcategory	Example
Subject	General overview	Can you give me some information about cancer?
	Differential diagnosis	How do you know when it's cancer and when it's just a benign growth?
	Therapy/treatment	What is the best therapy for autism?
	Other information resource referral	I'm looking for the book on who are the best doctors.
	Hospital/physician referral	I'm looking for the best doctor in Ames, Iowa, to treat my little boy.
	Diagnostic testing	What is a MRI and what does it tell the doctor?
	Pathophysiology	Why are men with cystic fibrosis usually unable to father children?
	Other	How many people in the U.S. lived 5 years after diagnosis with melanoma?

(Cont'd.)

	Figure 4-5: D'Alessandro's Taxonomy *(Continued)*	
Category	Subcategory	Example
	Not appropriate or indeterminate	Where can I meet other parents of children with Asperger's Syndrrome?
Medical area	Neurology/neurosurgery	These subcategories are all medical specialties; each question was indexed by D'Alessandro et al. as relating to a particular specialty.
	Allergy/pulmonary	
	Orthopedics/podiatry	
	Gastroenterology	
	Hematology/oncology	
	Cardiology/ cardiovascular surgery	
	Neonatalogy	
	General pediatric surgery	
	Nephrology/urology	
	Radiology	
	Genetics	
	All other specialties	
	Not appropriate or indeterminate	

(Based on information from "A Proposed Solution for Addressing the Challenge of Patient Cries for Help through an Analysis of Unsolicited Electronic Mail," published in the 2000 issue of *Pediatrics*.)

author's opinion) and also added the Support category to categorize an extremely common type of question encountered in this dataset: The "Are there more people out there like me?" request for support and similarity.

The fear of the medical question appears to be very much alive on the World Wide Web. A sorting mechanism that allows the truly problematic reference question—"Do I have cancer?" from the answerable reference question—"Where are online support groups about cancer?" could help virtual reference services meet the needs of healthcare consumer patrons. It is this author's hope that in future research, the proposed Triage Taxonomy can be field-tested and customized for use by virtual reference services wishing to address the urgent and emergent needs for healthcare information.

Figure 4-6: Bhavani's Taxonomy

Category	Definition	Example
Disease Type	General questions related to a certain disease type	I need all the information you have about melanoma.
Terminology	Broad terminology question	What does "staging" mean when the doctor talks about cancer?
Comparative	Question on comparison of two (or more) concepts	Which is worse, basal cell skin cancer or melanoma?
Definition	Definition of a disease term	What does "melanoma" mean?
Association	Relationship between two or more concepts	Does getting a lot of sunburns as a child mean you get melanoma later?
Risk/ Prevention	General questions about risk or prevention	How can I prevent my children from getting melanoma?
Risk Statistical	Statistics about risk or prevention	How many people in the U.S. had melanoma last year?
Specific Risk	Role of a specific risk or prevention factor	What are the effects of ultraviolet radiation?
Diagnosis	General question related to a certain disease diagnosis	How do they know when a person has melanoma?
Self-examination	Detection of a certain disease based on a self-description	I have a mole on my arm that looks like this. . . . Does this mean I have melanoma?
Doctor's exam	Issues related to a doctor's examination of a certain disease	Why does my doctor do an examination of my skin?
Treatment	General question related to disease treatment	Is chemotherapy effective against melanoma?
Test	Issues related to the procedure or result of the test for a certain disease	My white blood cell count was . . . my last checkup. Does this mean I have melanoma?
Prognosis	General question related to a certain disease prognosis	Do people live a long time after being diagnosed with melanoma?
Prognosis Statistical	Statistics about prognosis	How many people in the U.S. lived 5 years after diagnosis with melanoma?

Figure 4-7: The Triage Taxonomy

Category	Source taxonomy
Diagnosis Including differential diagnosis, symptoms	Roter D'Alessandro
Diagnostic testing	D'Alessandro
Epidemiology Including statistics about prevalence	Roter D'Alessandro
Etiology	Roter
General overview Including request for definitions	D'Alessandro
Wellness	Roter
Hospital/physician referral	D'Alessandro
Information resource referral	D'Alessandro
Medication	Roter
Prevention	Roter
Prognosis	Roter
Support	D'Alessandro
Treatment	Roter D'Alessandro

References

Alloway, Catherine Suyak, and L. Salisbury. 1983. "Issues in Consumer Health Information Services." *RQ* 23, no. 2: 143–149.

Bhavnani, Suresh K., Christopher K. Bichakjian, J. L. Schwartz, V. J. Strecher, R. L. Dunn, T. M. Johnson, and X. Lu. 2002. "Getting Patients to the Right Healthcare Sources: From Real-World Questions to Strategy Hubs." *Proceedings of the AMIA Symposium:* 51–55.

D'Alessandro, Donna M. 2000. "A Proposed Solution for Addressing the Challenge of Patient Cries for Help through an Analysis of Unsolicited Electronic Mail." *Pediatrics* 105, no. 6: E74.

Dewdney, P., Joanne Gard Marshall, and M. Tiamiyu. 1991. "A Comparison of Legal and Health Information Services in Public Libraries." *RQ* 3, no. 2: 185–196.

Farlow, John W. 1921. "The Relation of the Large Medical Library to the Community." *Bulletin of the Medical Library Association* 6, no. 4: 2–4.

Forsythe, Diana E., Bruce G. Buchanan, Jerome A. Osheroff, and Randolph A. Miller. 1992. "Expanding the Concept of Medical Information: An Observational Study of Physicians' Information Needs." *Computers in Biomedical Research* 25: 181–200.

Fox, Susannah, and Lee Rainie. "The Online Health Care Revolution: How the Web Helps Americans Take Better Care of Themselves." Washington, DC: Pew Internet & American Life Project (November 2000). Available: http://207.21.232.103/PPF/r/26/report_ display.asp

Fox, Susannah. "Health Information Online." Washington, DC: Pew Internet & American Life Project (May 2005). Available: www.pewinternet.org/PPF/c/5/topics.asp

Gillaspy, Mary L. 2000. "Starting a Consumer Health Information Service in a Public Library." *Public Library Quarterly* 18, nos. 3/4: 5–19.

Graesser, Arthur C. 1994. "Question Asking and Answering." In *Handbook of Psycholinguistics*, edited by M. A. Gerbsbacher. San Diego, CA: Academic Press.

Greenberg, Stephen J. 1997. "The 'Dreadful Visitation': Public Health and Public Awareness in Seventeenth-Century London." *Bulletin of the Medical Library Association* 85, no. 4: 391–401.

Horrigan, John, and Lee Rainie. "Counting on the Internet: Most Expect to Find Information Online/Most Find the Information They Seek/Many Now Turn to the Internet First." Washington, DC: Pew Internet & American Life Project (December 2002). Available: www.pewinternet.org/PPF/r/80/report_display.asp

Internet Public Library. "Privacy Statement." Ann Arbor, MI: Internet Public Library (2005). Available: www.ipl.org/div/about/privacy.html

Katz, William A. 1982. *Introduction to Reference Work*. New York: McGraw-Hill.

Reference and User Services Association, American Library Association. 2001. "Guidelines for Medical, Legal, and Business Information Service Responses (RUSA Guidelines)." *Reference & User Services Quarterly* 41, no. 2: 111–113.

Roter, Debra L. 1984. "Patient Question Asking and Answering." *Health Psychology* 3: 395–409.

Rubin, Rhea Joyce. 1983. "Public Access to Health Information: A Librarian's Response." *RQ* 22, no. 4: 409–410.

Simpson, John, and Edmund Weiner, eds. 1989. *Oxford English Dictionary*. 2nd ed. Oxford: Oxford University Press.

VRD. "AskA+ Locator: By subject" Syracuse, NY: Virtual Reference Desk Project (2005). Available: www.vrd.org/locator/subject.shtml

White, Marilyn D. 2000. "Questioning Behavior on an Electronic List." *Library Quarterly* 70, no. 3: 302–334.

Williams, M. Dawn, Kimbra Wilder Gish, Nunzia B. Guise, and Nila A. Sathe. 2001. "The Patient Informatics Consult Service (PICS): An Approach for a Patient-Centered Service." *Bulletin of the Medical Library Association* 89, no. 2: 185–193.

Williams, Raymond. 1934. "Changing Fashions and Habits in Medical Literature." *Bulletin of the Medical Library Association* 23, no. 2: 93–100.

Wood, Sandra. 1991. "Public Services Ethics in Health Sciences Libraries." *Library Trends* 40, no. 2: 244–257.

Chapter 5

The Evolving Role of Reference Librarians in the Health Sciences Environment

Gabriel R. Rios

Overview

Academic health sciences environments continue to change and evolve at an astronomical pace. The changes have had a significant impact on the provision of reference library services for health sciences clientele including clinicians, faculty, staff, and students.

In the changing work environment, health sciences reference librarians have adopted new roles:

- liaison
- information technology coach
- online architect

As the work environment continues to evolve, other challenges must be met:

- space utilization
- trends in education for the health professions
- access to e-resources
- visibility and marketing
- managing information overload

Although the role of reference librarian has changed, many core threads to reference librarianship remain.

Introduction and Background

One of the most significant guiding documents in health sciences libraries is the Association of Academic Health Sciences Libraries' *Building on Success, Charting the Future of Knowledge Management within the Academic Health Center* (AAHSL, 2003). This document emphasizes the library's role as an integral part of the clinical, education, research, and community service missions of academic health centers.

In preparing to write this chapter, the author reread the *Charting the Future* document and also examined numerous health sciences reference librarian job descriptions from the mid-1990s and from today. At first glance, he found that many of the tasks librarians performed in the mid-1990s, such as reference assistance and bibliographic instruction, were similar to the tasks performed today. One of the most remarkable differences is that librarians' practice environment has changed greatly due to the emergence of the Internet and access to online journals. From the first online journal title for health sciences debuting in 1994 to the several thousand journal titles available today, online journals have changed reference services and the jobs of reference librarians in many ways (Killion, 1994). Online journals have freed the library from the perception of being accessible from a single location by creating a digital library, or library without walls.

Responding to these changes, health sciences reference librarians practicing in digital libraries have adopted new roles to accommodate their changing environments, similar to the roles described by Stephen Pinfield in his article "Managing Electronic Library Services: Current Issues in UK Higher Education Institutions" (2001).

Liaison

Liaisons to user groups in the health sciences environment are essential to providing reference and information services. Liaisons serve as a conduit for two-way communication, allowing librarians to establish better communication channels, customize collection development and management, and develop a collaborative relationship between the library and each targeted department or user group.

The most established liaison activity is the clinical librarian. Clinical librarian programs started in the 1970s and were designed to provide quality-filtered, knowledge-based information to clinicians at the point of care to improve patient outcomes (Lamb, 1982). From this activity, a number of variations of this theme emerged, including the role of Informationist—evidence educator, and consumer health librarian (Homan and McGowan, 2002). Today, liaisons work with any department or user group in the health sciences setting. The majority of their interactions can occur on location with the user group and not in the library.

The Informationist concept describes someone that would be a member of the health care team, responsible to clinical staff. This person would have subject knowledge and the primary responsibility of bridging the gap between a caregiver's and a patient's information needs by providing access to the best information resources. Health sciences reference librarians with additional subject expertise are most effective in this role.

The evidence educator takes bibliographic instruction to the next level. Evidence educators tend to be integral to health sciences curricula. They teach users how to find and interpret heath sciences evidence. In a sense, evidence educators enable current and future health care professionals with the lifelong learning skills they need to improve patient outcomes.

Consumer health librarians arose from the increasing needs of patients and consumers to be better informed about their healthcare. Many academic health centers provide patient education services, and consumer health librarians develop and manage collections intended for patients and consumers. Furthermore, some consumer health librarians engage the community by providing health information at health and wellness fairs.

Many beneficial side effects occur through liaison activities, including:

- reference librarians have a better understanding of specific user group needs
- reference librarians have a better subject knowledge and expertise
- reference librarians are seen as part of the health care team
- libraries are seen as more accessible and relevant to user groups

Liaison programs also have the potential to assist with asking for financial support from the parent institution.

Information Technology Coach

Emerging technologies create an almost continuous state of change in libraries and information centers. From accessing online collections 24/7 to using Personal Digital Assistants (PDAs) and digital file players like iPods as information storage and retrieval tools, technology continues to influence the reference library environment.

Reference librarians have an increased role as supporters of technology. In addition to the number of questions asked about the public computers, one of the most frequently asked questions at a reference desk is, "How do I access journals from home?" A minimum level of technical knowledge is required at the reference desk to answer questions such as this one.

Reference librarians also have embraced roles using new information technologies such as PDAs and iPods. The academic health sciences library is the ideal digital incubator for testing technologies that deliver health information. Health sciences curricula, library vendors, and the current generation of millennials have helped initiate new roles for reference librarians, such as the PDA librarian. PDA users have access to library products, clinical tools, and practice guidelines. Reference librarians in this role are confident users of technology and are able to support library products with PDAs, iPods, or other appropriate technologies.

Online Architect

Reference librarians still organize resources and perform collection development activities; however, most of those functions are now Web-centric. A recent trend in libraries is to create user-driven Web experiences for specific user groups. The user-driven Web experience is also called a "portal." Portals are designed to meet most, if not all, of the information needs of the targeted user group. The Web presence is extremely important to the reference librarian since it is often the only point of contact for some remote library users.

Challenges

Reference librarians continue to rethink their roles as new challenges arise. These include space utilization and planning, trends in health professions education, access to e-resources, visibility and marketing, and managing information overload.

Space continues to challenge the role of reference libarians. The use of library space has changed as a result of the growing digital library. Gate counts have declined, but responsibilities to users have not decreased. Parent institution perceptions of library space have encouraged librarians to examine new ways to create an environment of teaching and learning. This environment can include subject-specific pods, or collaboratories.

Trends in health professions education continue to require changes in the roles of reference librarians. Several curricula have gradually decreased the actual amount of in-class lecture time. The library component is often one of the lectures that are cut when class time is at a premium. Reference librarians are resourceful and continue to explore virtual and noncompulsory classes for students to receive needed instruction.

E-resources, including online journals, are a blessing and a curse. Reference librarians enjoy the ubiquitous access to journal titles; however, that access sometimes comes at a price. It is not uncommon for an online resource to be unavailable, for a number of reasons. There also are challenges created when a library has a single title with specific years available from several different online vendors. Reference librarians continue to organize and examine new approaches to increase accessibility to online journals such as open URL resolvers.

Visibility and marketing are as much an opportunity as a challenge. As mentioned earlier, reference librarians have taken liaison roles that require them to be visible by attending meetings and being available at the user group's practice site. Reference librarians also are taking a proactive approach to marketing by making the library relevant to the targeted user group.

Information overload is a reality reference librarians will always need to manage. Today's users have the expectation of receiving an article or resource instantaneously. It is not atypical for academic health centers to have access to several thousand online journal titles, books, and databases. Reference librarians must critically analyze information resources to ensure that they are using the right tool for the job.

The Future

Reference librarian roles must always be flexible. As technology continues to impact our practice environment, librarians will continue to seek new ways to understand information-seeking behaviors and integrate "just-in-time" learning in the health sciences user environment. The role of reference librarians has changed in many ways over the past 10 years, but there are still many common threads that remain core to reference librarianship.

References

Association of Academic Health Sciences Libraries Charting the Future Task Force. 2003. "Building on Success: Charting the Future of Knowledge Management within the Academic Health Center." Seattle, WA: The Association of Academic Health Sciences Libraries. Available: www.aahsl.org/document/ ACF20BE.pdf (accessed May 2006).

Homan, J. Michael, and Julie J. McGowan. 2002. "The Medical Library Association: Promoting New Roles for Health Information Professionals." *Journal of the Medical Library Association* 90, no. 1: 80–85.

Killion, Vicki J. 1994. "Information Resources for Nursing Research: The Sigma Theta Tau International Electronic Library and Online Journal." *Medical Reference Services Quarterly* 13, no. 3: 1–17.

Lamb, Gertrude. 1982. "A Decade of Clinical Librarianship." *Clinical Librarian Quarterly* 1: 2–4.

Pinfield, Stephen. 2001. "Managing Electronic Library Services: Current Issues in UK Higher Education Institutions" Bath: *Ariadne* 29 (May 2006). Available: www. ariadne.ac.uk/issue29/pinfield/intro. html

Part III

Ongoing
Improvement

Examining Interpersonal Communication in Virtual Reference Encounters: The Library LAWLINE Consortium

Marie L. Radford

Overview

Certain aspects of interpersonal communication are critical in successful face-to-face (FtF) reference interactions. This study investigated communication in chat reference interactions. The author analyzed a random sample of 113 chat reference transcripts from Library LAWLINE, a regional chat reference consortium of law libraries.

Her analysis revealed that a wide range of interpersonal skills important to FtF reference success are present (although modified) in the chat environment. The study identified positive and negative behaviors facilitating and hindering communication.

Introduction and Background

This chapter describes the analysis of 113 transcripts from the Library LAWLINE: Live Assistance with Legal Information in the North East consortium (Matheson, 2004).[1] This study continues a research agenda that investigates the interpersonal communication aspects of virtual (chat) reference encounters. A pilot study was conducted with 44 transcripts from the S.S. Green Award, courtesy of LSSI (Radford, 2003). The pilot study was followed by an analysis of 245 transcripts from Maryland AskUsNow!, a statewide consortium (Radford, 2006b). To explore whether the findings from the statewide consortium transcript

---

[1] The author wishes to express deep appreciation to Tracy Thompson, Executive Director of the New England Law Library Consortia (NELLCO), for her permission to use these transcripts, for pulling the random sample, and cleansing identifying information from them.

analysis would be similar to that of a specialized service, Library LAWLINE transcripts were analyzed regarding interpersonal communication strategies.[2]

Literature Review

Arnold and Kaske (2005) and Nilsen (2004) review research on chat reference services, as does Pomerantz (2005), who also details a research agenda for future investigations of virtual reference services. Radford (2006a) reviews the pertinent library literature as well as the computer-mediated communication literature, which enhances understanding of interpersonal aspects in the chat environment.

A review of the literature on electronic reference in law libraries revealed that little has been published in this area. Selby (1999) describes an e-mail reference service at the University of Virginia's Law Library. Balleste and Russell (2003) write a descriptive piece from the perspective of library administrators on implementation of a chat service by a consortium of Florida's St. Thomas University Law Library and Nova Southeastern University Law Library, which began in 2002. They discuss features of the different chat services and decision points in system implementation. Similarly, Matheson (2004) details the origins of the Library LAWLINE service in New England (which provided the transcripts for the present analysis). He also describes the decision-making process for the collaborative service that began as a "joint project of 19 libraries from seven states" (Matheson, 2004: 102). Matheson chronicles the decision to use 24/7 software, the negotiations regarding service, policies, use of licensed resources, training, promotion, evaluation, and staffing designs. He notes: "The element of the service that presented the biggest challenge was the collaboration between public and academic law libraries— libraries that have different, sometimes very different patron bases and service models" (Matheson, 2004: 102). Matheson covers the service start-up and the pilot project that ran from September 2002 to August 2003, with 15 academic and four non-academic libraries participating in sharing 56 hours of chat service per week, including eight hours on the weekends. He ends with a discussion of recommendations for other libraries considering consortial chat services.

Following the pilot project, the regular service ran from September 2003 to August 2005, operating 45 hours per week, six days per week (no Saturday service). The service had a healthy volume of questions, approximately 200 per month, but because of the predominance of academic libraries in the consortium, the target audience had been law students needing assistance with course assignments. "Statistics showed that academic patrons were the least frequent users of the service" (Matheson, 2004: 109). The majority of those using the service were members of the public with real-life questions concerning domestic issues, housing law, motor vehicle infractions, and other personal legal queries.

---

[2] The author thanks Denise Feder, Graduate Assistant, MLIS student from Rutgers University, School of Communication, Information, and Library Studies, for her help in data coding and analysis and for her considerable Excel expertise.

When Library LAWLINE ceased operation in August of 2005, eight law libraries had remained in the consortium: six academic and two public. After the dissolution of Library LAWLINE, two libraries still continued the service serving a similar patron base. An additional factor in the breakup of the consortium was an impending change in software in the summer of 2005, when 24/7 was acquired by OCLC, Online Computer Library Center, Inc., which would have required significant retraining efforts and perhaps a change in vendors. Also, there were sporadic but troubling software problems and staff disappointment in co-browsing features. Library LAWLINE provided clients with a pop-up client survey that received overwhelmingly positive results. "About eight in ten patrons were happy with the service and would use it again" (Matheson, 2004: 112).

It is noteworthy that a comprehensive survey article (Grey, 2005) describes 65 important articles in legal reference, yet includes no articles on virtual reference in the law library, although she includes a few articles (e.g., Ross, 2003) that cover general skills for virtual as well as face-to-face (FtF) reference practitioners. No published research studies focusing on transcript analysis of law library chat encounters or using communication theory as a foundation of the type that this research project addresses were found.

Research Questions

As in previous research studies of interpersonal communication dimensions in chat reference transcripts by this author, the following research questions were explored:

1. What relational dimensions are present in chat reference transcripts?
2. Are there differences in the relational dimensions/patterns of chat clients and librarians? If so, what are they?
3. How do clients and librarians compensate for lack of nonverbal cues in chat reference?
4. What is the relationship between content and relational dimensions in determining the quality of chat reference encounters?

Method

Ten Library LAWLINE transcripts per month were randomly selected for a total of 120 transcripts from a population of 2,400. Of these, 113 were found to be useable, as the remaining seven were system tests. All transcripts were cleansed of any identification information such as names, IP addresses, and e-mail addresses. All discourse in the transcripts was coded except for pre-written "scripts," such as "A librarian will be with you in about 2 minutes."

The transcripts were qualitatively analyzed through repeated reading, identification, comparison, and categorization of issues, patterns, and themes. This coding method and category scheme was developed in qualitative research involving interviews and observation in academic libraries (see Radford, 1993, 1999) and in previous analyses of chat transcripts (see Radford,

2006a, 2006b). Using the theoretical framework of Watzlawick, Beavin and Jackson (1967) focus was placed on investigation of relational (i.e., interpersonal, affect-oriented, socioemotional) aspects of the transcripts to address the research questions. It is to be noted that content/task dimensions centering on whether the answer was correct or complete, although recognized as critically important in evaluation of chat reference, were not analyzed in this project. The unit of analysis is a conversational turn and, in many cases, more than one category may appear per conversational turn, and turns can be parsed into several lines. Counts and percentages of the presence and numbers of occurrences of categories were carefully tracked.

Results

Prior research investigating interpersonal communication in chat reference (Radford, 2006a, 2006b) found that a variety of interpersonal aspects important to traditional, face-to-face reference success are found (although somewhat modified) in chat reference transcripts. These interpersonal dimensions include: strategies for rapport building, representation of nonverbal cues, techniques for relationship development, indications of deference, respect, face-saving, greeting rituals, and closing rituals. See Appendix 6A for the Library LAWLINE Category Scheme which built upon the findings from the Green Award pilot and Maryland AskUsNow! study results.

Two major themes—relational facilitators and relational barriers—were found to be present for both librarians and clients in the Library LAWLINE transcripts (see also Radford, 1993, 1999, 2006a, 2006b). Relational facilitators are interpersonal aspects of the chat conversation that have a positive impact on the interaction and that enhance communication (see Radford, 1993, 1999, 2006a). Relational barriers are relational aspects that have a negative impact on the interaction and that impede communication (see Radford, 1993, 1999, 2006a).

Relational Facilitators

Within the relational facilitators theme, five sub-themes were found for both librarians and Library LAWLINE clients: rapport building, deference, rerepresentation of nonverbal cues, closing ritual, and greeting ritual. "Rerepresentation" is a term used in computer-mediated communication literature to denote text or font for replacing nonverbal communication cues. The following transcript illustrates positive relational dimensions for both librarian and client.

This transcript starts with the user asking the question in a deferential way that concludes with a "thank you" in line 1 (CF1A).[3] The librarian quickly makes a disclaimer in line 4 (LB2C), but offers to find a local resource that

---

[3] Codes in parentheses refer to Appendix A Classification Scheme for Interpersonal Communication in Library LAWLINE Consortium Chat Reference Transcripts codes, so (LB1C) refers to LB—Librarian Barrier; 1—Relational Disconnect/Failure to Build Rapport; C—Limits Time.

Excerpt from Transcript #011

1   Client: If you have historical sets of state statutes and local laws...can you answer this: What necessary procedures had to be followed in 1952 for an adoption to be legal. What were the procedural steps for NY state? Also the current stautes as well that may effect an adoption in 1952 maybe Montgomery Co or Albany Co. thank you.

2   [A librarian will be with you in about a minute.]

3   [A librarian has joined the session.]

4   Librarian: This question goes beyond the scope of the service the Library Lawline provides. I can try to help you find a local resource that you could use to research this issue.

5   C: That would be great. I'm in [another state] and I'm having trouble getting the info about NY state laws, then and now!

      [text omitted]

6   L: Ok. This may take me a few minutes.

      [text omitted]

7   L: OK: it looks like the University of XX Law Library has the historical NY state statutes. However, its always a good idea to call ahead and make sure—it's a little tough to confirm from their catalog.

      [text omitted]

8   L: For current procedure, there is probably something online

9   C: Sounds great. Where online do I go for current

10   [Web page sent]

11 L: The links on this page may help.

      [text omitted]

12   [Web page sent]

13 C: your great! Thanks for all your assistance

14 L: You're welcome—does that address all your questions?

15 C: Yes, for now.

16 L: Good luck then!

17   [user has closed this session]

---

the user can use to do his/her research which is reassuring (LF1D). The client expresses deference in the form of enthusiasm ("That would be great," "Sounds great," "Your [sic] great!" CFIG), in lines 5, 9, and 13 in response to the librarian's suggestions and pushed Web pages. The client again thanks the librarian in line 13 (CF1A), and the librarian provides a polite "You're welcome" in response (LF2A). Positive closure is achieved in lines 14, when the librarian asks "does that address all your questions?" and with the unscripted closing ritual in line 16, "Good luck then!" with the exclamation point for additional emphasis (LF5B, LF3B).

Relational Barriers

Within the relational barriers theme, two sub-themes were found for librarians (negative closure and relational disconnect/failure to build rapport) and clients (closing problems—signing off abruptly and relational disconnect/failure to build rapport). Definitions of themes and sub-themes draw upon the work of Goffman (1956, 1972), Radford (1993, 1996, 1999), and Ross and Dewdney (1998) and are described in Radford (2006a). The excerpt below from a transcript about a motor vehicle regulation in the state of Massachusetts is included below because it provides examples of both facilitators and barriers. No corrections have been made to misspellings or grammatical errors.

Excerpt from Transcript #012

1   Client: How low can your car be before its against the law in massachusetts?

2   [A librarian will be with you in about 2 minutes.]

3   [A librarian has joined the session.]

4   Librarian: I have someone else on the line as well, but could you clarify your question. Do you mean how long can you have a car registered in another state in Massachusetts before you are required to change your registration to Massachusetts?

5   C: No

6   C: How low (in terms of height) can you car be before it is against the law?

7   L: You mean like, how short your tires are?

8   C: No. the car itself. From the ground.

9   L: You mean to the top of the car? The tires obviously touch the ground or your wouldn't go.

10   C: From the bottom to the ground.

11   L: You mean like they are talking about in this article?

12   [Web page sent]

13   C: So whats the exact height regulation?

14   L: Now that I understand the question, I'll try to look it up. This will take a minute or two, at least, unless I'm real lucky.

15   C: Ok. Thanks.

16   L: This might be the text you want

17   [text sent]

18   L: It comes from 540 CMR 4.04

19   C: Now can you get your car impounded if the car is altered more than 2 inches?

20   L: This might also be applicable and the section you really need.

21   [Web page sent]

22   L: I'm not allowed to give legal advice, just research help

Excerpt from Transcript #012 *(Continued)*

23 L: I also don't type or spell well, but that's another story.

24 C: lol

25 C: I was trying to type everything correctly myself as well.

[text omitted]

26 C: I just want to know can your car be impounded . . . like what are the infractions?

27 L: I am going off duty now—actually a half hour ago. Can I transfer you to another librarian?

28 [you have been transferred to library xxx]

29 [A librarian has joined the session]

30 [patron—had disconnected]

Transcript 012 starts with an awkward beginning. In line 4, above the librarian tells the client that someone else is on the line (LB1C). The librarian asks for clarification of the question, but seems distracted, perhaps by the other client(s) on the line. The librarian admits that he/she finally understands the question in line 14 and also builds some rapport with the user by being deferential and adding some humor: "I'll try to look it up. This will take a minute or two, at least, (see code LF2A) unless I am real lucky" (see code LF1H). The client responds with a reassuring and deferential "Ok. Thanks" (see codes CF2A, CF1A).

In line 19, the client asks a pointed question about whether the car can be impounded, and the librarian gives a disclaimer: "I'm not allowed to give legle [sic] advice, just research help" (LB2C) but softens the disclaimer in the next line with additional rapport-building humor: "I also don't type or spell well, but that's another story." The client rewards this with "lol," which translates to "laughing out loud" (CF4A). Contrast this with the excerpt from transcript 11, line 4 "This question goes beyond the scope of the service the Library Lawline provides. I can try to help you find a local resource that you could use to research this issue." In both cases, a disclaimer is given, and, in both cases the disclaimer is softened.

The client in transcript 12 exhibits empathy in line 25: "I was trying to type everything correctly myself as well" (CF2A). After some more back-and-forth, the client again returns to the pointed question about whether the car can be impounded, and the librarian uses a negative closure strategy, in line 27, limiting time (LB1C) and transferring the client to another librarian, line 28, without giving the deference to the client in waiting for him/her to agree to this transfer. The client signs off abruptly, in response to this abrupt transfer in line 30. Although the librarian had built positive rapport with the user in the middle of the transcript, the abrupt departure is a barrier to positive communication.

Discussion

As can be seen in the Category Scheme (Appendix 6A), and in the excerpt from transcript 11 above, in the area of librarian relational facilitators, rapport building was the largest category, found in 81 (72 percent) of the transcripts. Several new categories were identified in this section that had not been identified in the Green Award or Maryland AskUsNow! transcripts, including LF2A, which involves the librarian showing deference to the client by asking for the client to be patient. This category included statements like that of transcript 12, line 14, above "This will take a minute or two, at least, unless I'm real lucky." This deference to the client shows that the librarian values the client's time and does not want the client to become impatient since law questions may be quite involved, requiring more than mere seconds to retrieve from the Web or from law books. This strategy is an excellent method to help decrease the number of impatient clients or those who disappear suddenly because they became frustrated with waiting. In the area of LF3, Closing Ritual, LF3 B, C, and D are new categories. These involve the librarian inviting the client to return if necessary (14 transcripts, 12 percent), offering to continue searching and e-mail the answer (8, 12 percent), and making sure that the client has no more questions (6, 5 percent). The presence of these facilitators again reflects the lengthy nature of many law questions that require followup beyond what can be done quickly in the chat environment.

In the area of client relational facilitators, deference to the librarian was the largest category, with 86 (76 percent) of the transcripts coded to reflect client respect for the librarian. Eighty (70 percent) of the clients thanked the librarian during the course of the session, including the client in transcript 12, line 15, above. Clients reflected the professional tone of the librarians, and so informal language was seen in only 11 (10 percent) of the transcripts.

Although 38 (34 percent) of the librarians ended the interactions on a very positive note with unscripted closing rituals, 34 (30 percent) of the transcripts were coded with instances of negative closure. Twenty-four (21 percent) included disclaimers such as transcript 11, line four: "This question goes beyond the scope of the service the Library Lawline provides," and transcript 12, line 22: "I'm not allowed to give legle [sic] advice, just research help." These disclaimers exemplify the law librarian's goal of not engaging in the Unauthorized Practice of Law (UPL). Grey's (2005) bibliography on legal reference service highlights the seriousness of this professional issue and provides annotations of several articles dealing with this topic (Brown, 1994; Condon, 2001; Mosley, 1995; Rice 1990; Trosow, 2001; Whisner, 1999) and an annotated bibliography of 25 items on UPL (Healey, 2002). Arant and Carpenter (1999) provide guidelines to help law librarians determine where the line is between providing reference versus legal advice.

Law librarians are careful not to step over this line and inform clients of these boundaries, as seen in these Library LAWLINE transcripts. Within the communication theory framework and a client-centered perspective, it is recommended that law librarians in chat environments treat this referral to the client's lawyer like any other referral. For example, the librarian could have responded in transcript 12 by saying: " Hmmm...you need to ask your lawyer that question" or "Although your question is one that this service is unable to answer, here is the Web site URL (or phone number) for a legal aid organization that provides pro bono legal help and could perhaps answer your question." Matheson (2004: 111) notes that educating clients about the limits of the service was important during the pilot phase, and that some Library LAWLINE clients "thought that they would be getting free legal advice (we became quite adept at referring patrons to free and low-cost legal service information)."

Looking at the relational barriers found for clients, despite the librarians frequently asking clients to be patient while they conducted searches, 38 (34 percent) of the clients signed off abruptly without any explanation, including the client in transcript 12, line 30. It is possible that some of these disappearing clients could have been disconnected while experiencing technical problems. Clients of Library LAWLINE were, for the most part, polite and willing to wait for their information, appreciative of the librarian's expertise, and understanding of the limitations of time pressure and/or professional discretion.

Conclusion

These results are significant in that they represent the first in-depth analysis of transcripts from a specialized, law library consortium. It would be fruitful to examine transcripts from an array of university, corporate, statewide, and national VR services to see the differences and similarity in interpersonal communication patterns. It is also important to follow up on these findings to see, for example, the impact of staff education in interpersonal aspects of chat, and in trying different approaches to educating clients about the need for reference librarians to avoid the Unauthorized Practice of Law.

This research demonstrates that applying communication theory to the analysis of virtual reference transcripts provides valuable insights. Further, it can help librarians understand how each chat interaction is unique, requiring a flexible set of guidelines that can be applied to enhance the experience of both client and librarian. It is hoped that future research projects will continue to build on these findings to extend knowledge and understanding of the virtual reference encounter in a variety of types of services.

Appendix 6A

Classification Scheme for Interpersonal Communication in Library LAWLINE Consortium Chat Reference Transcripts

Relational Facilitators—Librarians—Frequency Order   **(N=113 Transcripts)**

LF 1 Rapport Building–81 (72 percent)
  A. Seeking reassurance/confirmation/self-disclosure–53 (47 percent)
  B. Offering confirmation–40 (35 percent)
      1. Inclusion (e.g, let's . . . , why don't we do x)–39 (35 percent)
      2. Empathy–4 (4 percent)
      3. Approval–2 (2 percent)
  C. Self-disclosure–39 (29 percent)
      1. Offering personal opinion/advice/value judgment–39 (35 percent)
      2. Admitting lack of knowledge/at a loss as to where to search 17 (15 percent)
      3. Explaining search strategy–14 (12 percent)
      4. Providing information about self–14 (12 percent)
      5. Explaining technical problems–4 (4 percent)
  D. Offering reassurance–39 (35 percent)
      1. Encouraging remarks/praise–20 (18 percent)
      2. Enthusiastic remarks–4 (4 percent)
  E. Use of informal language–10 (9 percent)
  F. Humor–8 (7 percent)
  G. Interjections–7 (6 percent)
  H. Repair/self-correction–4 (4 percent)

LF 2 Deference 60 (50 percent)
  A. Asking for client to be patient–44 (39 percent)
  B. Use of polite expressions–30 (26 percent)
  C. Apology–13 (12 percent)
  D. Thanks–11 (10 percent)
  E. Use of self-deprecating remarks–2 (2 percent)

LF 3 Closing Ritual–55 (49 percent)
  A. Unscripted–36 (32 percent)
  B. Invites to return if necessary–14 (12 percent)
  C. Offers to continue searching & email answer–8 (7 percent)
  D. Makes sure client has no more questions–6 (5 percent)

LF 4 Greeting Ritual, Unscripted–51 (45 percent)

LF 5 Rerepresentation of Nonverbal Cues–37 (32 percent)
  A. Use of abbreviations (e. g., LOL)/alternative spelling–17 (15 percent)
  B. Uses ellipsis to indicate more to come–5 (13 percent)
  C. Punctuation for emphasis–15 (13 percent)
  D. Use of repeat punctuation (e.g., !!!)–1 (<1 percent)
  E. Spells out nonverbal behaviors (e.g., grin, wink wink, ha ha)–1 (<1 percent)

Note: Each number in parenthesis is the number of transcripts that exhibited the category. Numbers below the main categories (in bold) do not total since transcripts can exhibit more than one sub-category. Percentages are rounded to the nearest whole number. © Marie L. Radford, 2005.

Relational Facilitators—Client—Frequency Order   (N=113 Transcripts)

CF 1 Deference–86 (76 percent)
- A. Thanks–80 (70 percent)
- B. Agreement to try what is suggested/to wait–36 (32 percent)
- C. Use of praise, admiration–23 (20 percent)
- D. Expressions of enthusiasm–16 (14 percent)
- E. Use of polite expressions–14 (12 percent)
- F. Apology–9 (8 percent)
- G. Use of self-deprecating remarks–9 (8 percent)
- H. Suggesting strategy or explanation in tentative way–8 (7 percent)

CF 2 Rapport Building–69 (61 percent)
- A. Self-disclosure–44 (39 percent)
- B. Empathy/confirmation/reassurance–30 (26 percent)
- C. Seeking reassurance–26 (23 percent)
- D. Use of informal language–11 (10 percent)
- E. Repair/correction–9 (8 percent)
- F. Interjections–7 (6 percent)
- G. Humor–1 (<1 percent)

CF 3 Rerepresentation of NV Cues 45 (40 percent)
- A. Use of abbreviations (e.g., LOL)/Alpha-numeric shortcuts (e.g., L8R)–24 (21 percent)
- B. Use of ellipsis–16 (14 percent)
- C. Use of repeated punctuation (e.g., ???)–9 (8 percent)
- D. Punctuation for emphasis–5 (4 percent)
- E. Use of ALL CAPS–4 (4 percent)
- F. Alternative spelling–4 (4 percent)
- G. Emoticons–3 (3 percent)
- H. Spell out nonverbal behaviors (e.g. grin, wink wink, ha ha)–1 (<1 percent)

CF 4 Closing Ritual–40 (35 percent)
- A. Nonscripted–38 (34 percent)
- B. Explanation of signing off abruptly–2 (2 percent)

CF 5 Greeting Ritual–18 (15 percent)

Note: Each number in parenthesis is the number of transcripts that exhibited the category. Numbers below the main categories (in bold) do not total since transcripts can exhibit more than one sub-category. Percentages are rounded to the nearest whole number. © Marie L. Radford, 2005.

Relational Barriers—Librarian—Frequency Order   (N=113 Transcripts)

LB 1 Negative Closure–34 (30 percent)
- A. Disclaimer–24 (21 percent)
- B. Abrupt ending–12 (11 percent)
- C. Ignoring cues that client wants more help–5 (4 percent)
- D. Premature/Attempted Closing–1 (<1 percent)
- E. Premature referral–1 (<1 percent)

LB 2 Relational Disconnect/Failure to Build Rapport–22 (19 percent)
- A. Disconfirming–8 (7 percent)
- B. Limits time–7 (6 percent)

C. Failing to offer reassurance–4 (4 percent)
D. Ignoring client self-disclosure–4 (4 percent)
E. Lack of attention – Ignoring question–2 (2 percent)
F. Misunderstands client's question–1 (<1 percent)
G. Inappropriate script/response–1 (<1 percent)
H. Condescending–1 (<1 percent)
I. Robotic answer–1 (<1 percent)

Relational Barriers—Clients—Frequency Order   **(N=113 Transcripts)**

CB 1 Closing Problems—Signing off abruptly–38 (34 percent)

CB 2 Relational Disconnect/Failure to Build Rapport–6 (5 percent)
A. Disconfirming (e.g., I already have that info.)–3 (3 percent)
B. Impatience–1 (<1 percent)
C. Failure/refusal to provide information when asked–1 (<1 percent)
D. Ignores librarian humor–1 (<1 percent)

Note: Each number in parenthesis is the number of transcripts that exhibited the category. Numbers below the main categories (in bold) do not total since transcripts can exhibit more than one sub-category. Percentages are rounded to the nearest whole number.

References

Arant, Wendy, and Brian Carpenter. 1999. "Where Is the Line? Legal Reference Service and the Unauthorized Practice of Law (UPL)—Some Guidelines That May Help." *Reference & User Services Quarterly* 38, no. 3 (Spring): 235–239.

Arnold, Julie, and Neal Kaske. 2005. "Evaluating the Quality of a Chat Service." *Portal: Libraries and the Academy* 5, no. 2: 177–193.

Balleste, Ray, and Gordon Russell. 2003. "Implementing Virtual Reference: Hollywood Technology in Real Life." *Computers in Libraries* 23, no. 4: 14–16.

Brown, Yvette. 1994. "From the Reference Desk to the Jail House: Unauthorized Practice of Law and Librarians." *Legal Reference Services Quarterly* 13, no. 4: 31–45.

Condon, Charles J. 2001. "How to Avoid the Unauthorized Practice of Law at the Reference Desk." *Legal Reference Services Quarterly* 19, no. 1/2: 165–179.

Goffman, E. 1956. "The Nature of Deference and Demeanor." *American Anthropologist* 58, no. 3: 475–499.

Goffman, E. 1972. *Relations in Public: Microstudies of the Public Order*. New York: Basic Books.

Grey, Debbie. 2005. "Legal Reference Services: An Annotated Bibliography." *Law Library Journal* 97, no. 3 (Summer): 537–564.

Healey, Paul. 2002. "Pro Se Users, Reference Liability, and the Unauthorized Practice of Law: Twenty-Five Selected Readings." *Law Library Journal* 94: 133–139.

Janes, Joseph. 2003. *Introduction to Reference Work in the Digital Age*. New York: Neal-Schuman.

Matheson, Scott. 2004. "Library LAWLINE: Collaborative Virtual Reference in a Special Library Consortium." *The Reference Librarian* 41, no. 85: 101–114.

Mosley, Madison M., Jr. 1995. "The Authorized Practice of Legal Reference Service." *Law Library Journal* 87 (Winter): 203–209.

Nilsen, Kirsty. 2004. "The Library Visit Study: User Experiences at the Virtual Reference Desk." *Information Research* 9, no. 2. Available: http://InformationR.net/ir/9-2/paper171.html

Pomerantz, Jeffrey. 2005. "A Conceptual Framework and Open Research Questions for Chat-Based Reference Service." *Journal of the American Society for Information Science and Technology* 56, no. 12: 1288–1302.

Radford, Marie L. 1996. "Communication Theory Applied to the Reference Encounter: An Analysis of Critical Incidents." *Library Quarterly* 66, no. 2: 123–137.

Radford, Marie L. 2006a. "Encountering Virtual Users: A Qualitative Investigation of Interpersonal Communication in Chat Reference." *Journal of the American Society for Information Science and Technology* 57, no. 8: 1046–1059.

Radford, Marie L. 2003. "In Synch? Evaluating Chat Reference Transcripts." Presented at the Virtual Reference Desk 5th Annual Digital Reference Conference, San Antonio, TX, November 17–18.

Radford, Marie L. 2006b. "Interpersonal Communication in Chat Reference: Encounters with Rude and Impatient Users." In *Creating a Reference Future: Proceedings of the Virtual Reference Desk Conference*, edited by D. Lankes, E. Abels, M. White, and S. Hague. New York: Neal-Schuman.

Radford, Marie L. 1999. "The Reference Encounter: Interpersonal Communication in the Academic Library." Chicago, IL: ACRL, A Division of the American Library Association.

Radford, Marie L. 1993. *Relational Aspects of Reference Interactions: A Qualitative Investigation of the Perceptions of Users and Librarians in the Academic Library.* Unpublished doctoral dissertation, Rutgers. DAI A54/07, 2368.

Rice, Michael E. 1990. "Reference Service Versus Unauthorized Legal Practice—Implications for the Canadian Reference Librarian." *Legal Reference Services Quarterly* 10, no. 1/2: 41–57.

Ross, Catherine S. 2003. "The Reference Interview: Why It Needs to Be Used in Every (Well, Almost Every) Reference Transaction." *Reference and User Services Quarterly* 42: 290–295.

Ross, Catherine S., and Patricia Dewdney. 1998. "Negative Closure: Strategies and Counter-Strategies in the Reference Transaction." *RUSQ* 38, no. 2 (Winter): 151–163.

Selby, Barbara. 1999. "Refdesk: UVa Law Library's Approach to E-mail Reference." *Virginia Libraries* 45, no. 2: 12–13.

Trosow, Samuel E. 2001. "Jurisdictional Disputes and the Unauthorized Practice of Law: New Challenges for Law Librarianship." *Legal Reference Services Quarterly* 20, no. 4: 1–18.

Walther, Joseph B., and Kyle P. D'Addario. 2001. "The IMpacts of Emoticons on Message Interpretation in Computer-Mediated Communication." *Social Science Computer Review* 19, no. 3: 342–347.

Watzlawick, Paul, Janet B. Beavin, and Don D. Jackson. 1967. *Pragmatics of Human Communication.* New York: Norton.

Whisner, Mary. 1999. "Golf Buddy Reference Questions." *Law Library Journal* 91: 413–416.

Chapter 7

Assessing Inappropriate Use: Learning from the AskColorado Experience

Jack Maness and Sarah Naper

Overview

A common complaint in the library community is that virtual reference services are routinely misused. How are "appropriate use" and "inappropriate use" defined? This chapter presents an analysis of two years of virtual reference use in AskColorado, one statewide collaborative service. The following questions are addressed:

- Does AskColorado's inappropriate behavior correlate strongly with inappropriate behavior measurements from other statewide virtual reference services?
- Has inappropriate behavior on AskColorado changed as the service has evolved?
- Are there trends in inappropriate behavior on AskColorado that can be identified?

The conclusion includes recommendations.

Introduction and Background

AskColorado is a statewide collaborative virtual reference service that includes membership from academic, public, school, and special libraries. The service's objective is to combine resources from libraries to provide a 24/7 online chat reference service that efficiently and effectively meets the information and learning needs of the state's residents. Since the service's inception in September 2003, AskColorado has proved to be a busy service, with a first year average of over 2,000 questions received per month. In the second year, usage more than doubled to an average of over 4,000 questions per month. In both years, K–12 students accounted for over 50 percent of total use, with much of this use during school hours. Patron exit surveys have yielded positive results,

91

with three out of four rating the service as excellent or good, indicating that the service was well liked.

Maintaining staff morale within a multi-type library collaborative is just as important as maintaining excellent service. Many librarians who work the service have experienced rude patrons, which make them question the value of the service. Yet, is inappropriate use really a significant part of the overall service, or is it only occasional misuse that colors staff perceptions?

With this question as an impetus, the service's Quality Assurance and Evaluation (QA&E) subcommittee was encouraged to conduct a study of inappropriate use. QA&E's charge within AskColorado's structure is to oversee quality using feedback and assessment to maintain high standards of reference service. The subcommittee regularly analyzes transaction transcripts to identify exemplary service and areas where improvement is needed.

Inspired by studies of inappropriate use in New Jersey by Peter Bromberg (2004) and in Maryland by Joseph Thompson (2005), and by a presentation delivered at the Virtual Reference Desk Conference in 2004 by Joseph Thompson and Marie Radford, committee members analyzed one week of transactions from each of the two years of service in an attempt to assess the extent of the problem and to seek trends that may contribute to the discovery of effective training measures for handling such inappropriate behavior.

Literature Review

Literature on two librarianship topics was reviewed: Virtual reference transaction analysis and inappropriate behavior in libraries. The former was reviewed as comprehensively as possible; the latter, for which there is a long history and wealth of literature, was limited to recent publications, corresponding to the advent of electronic services in libraries, generally from the mid-1990s to the present, as literature from this period was considered most pertinent to the issue at hand.

Research on the analysis of virtual reference transactions tended to fall in one of two categories: Research conducted in the aim of improving virtual reference services themselves and research conducted in order to gain an insight into the nature of reference services more generally. Research conducted for the sake of improving virtual reference and training staffers of such services included studies on communication in virtual environments (Radford and Thompson, 2004), models for analyzing transactions (Lee, 2004; Radford, 2003; Smyth, 2003), general overviews of the chat reference interview (Bobrowsky, Beck and Grant, 2005), and guidelines for using transcripts in staff training initiatives (Ward, 2003).

Other studies used Reference and User Services Association (RUSA) standards for reference practice to evaluate the quality of particular services (Kwon, 2004). Studies that analyzed virtual reference transcripts and made reference practice generalizations often cited the value of unobtrusive observation (Jensen, 2004), their use in comparing chat reference to e-mail reference (Lee, 2004), and the enormous implication that "[f]or the first time in our profession we have a growing body of written records of reference transactions to study" (Tennant, 2003: 38).

The literature on the inappropriate behavior of patrons in libraries was constrained to recent publications because, as several researchers noted, the nature of such behavior has changed with the advent of electronic library services (Blessinger, 2002; Borin, 2002; Peatling, 2002). Limiting the review to recent publications is intended to include only research related to the issue at hand: Inappropriate behavior within electronic library services. Though the consensus emphasized that the nature of such behavior has changed in the online environment, some of the same researchers noted that inappropriate behavior has always been a concern for libraries (Blessinger, 2002; Peatling, 2002). Other research suggested an increase in the magnitude of inappropriate behavior in recent years (Blessinger, 2002; Bullard, 2002). Peatling, however, noted that such "[e]ncounters with aggression and hostility are difficult to quantify" (Peatling, 2002: 40).

Much of the literature was pragmatic in nature, attempting to provide suggestions for dealing with rude or inappropriate behavior, and there was widespread agreement that defining "problem" behavior is difficult, and that doing so is rife with subjectivity (Chattoo, 2002; Chelton, 2002; Currie, 2002).

This study delves into the overlap between transcript analysis and inappropriate patron behavior, an area with a limited number of published works. Taylor and Porter (2002) deal almost exclusively with such behavior in virtual environments, accurately asserting: "Particularly when a library is initiating a new service, there may not be an easy mechanism for verifying legitimate users. There may even be a lack of desire to do so, since most new services get low use initially, and libraries may be trying to promote use in general" (Taylor and Porter, 2002: 171). Transcript analysis is a seemingly wonderful mechanism for verifying legitimate users, once the desire is in place, yet there are only two unpublished studies on this topic, both of which served as models for the AskColorado study. Peter Bromberg (2004) apparently originated the quantification of inappropriate use with his 2002 analysis of New Jersey's (Q&ANJ) transcripts. Thompson (2005) expanded Bromberg's model with his 2004 analysis of transcripts from Maryland's AskUsNow. Both of these initiatives involved statewide cooperative services, very similar to AskColorado.

Methodology

In devising our study, the subcommittee identified three research questions for exploration:

(R1) Does AskColorado's inappropriate behavior correlate strongly with inappropriate behavior measurements from other statewide virtual reference services?

(R2) Has inappropriate behavior on AskColorado changed as the service evolved?

(R3) Are there trends in inappropriate behavior on AskColorado that we can identify?

In determining how to code inappropriate use, at Bromberg's and Thompson's DigRef listserv postings of descriptions of their studies were consulted. (DigRef is an e-mail listserv dedicated to the exploration of "the growing area of digital reference services." More information is available at: www.vrd. org/Dig_Ref/dig_ref. shtml. DigRef archives, including the postings by both Bromberg and Thompson, are available at: http://finance.groups.yahoo.com/group/dig_ref/) In both cases, transcripts were reviewed for inappropriate use. Bromberg's study established a framework for reviewing appropriateness of interactions, classifying 509 transcripts into the following categories: (1) appropriate, (2) goofing around, and (3) inappropriate language. Thompson's review of 899 transcripts expanded Bromberg's framework slightly by adding the category of "hurried/rude," hence coding options included: (1) appropriate, (2) hurried/rude, (3) goofing around, and (4) inappropriate language.

Since the hope was to compare the inappropriate use of AskColorado with other state projects, the coding here is very similar to the previous studies. However, to minimize confusion, all non-appropriate use has been labeled "inappropriate" and subdivided into the following categories.

Goofing Around

The operating definition for this category was "Patron does not have a question or reference transaction; he/she often is just messing around with the software, typing nonsense characters, or asking tangential questions." In some cases, a patron may be on task, but also ask tangential questions like "Do you like pizza?" or "How old are you?" These were marked goofing around since this was, in fact, happening. Other transcripts in this category might include an initial question such as "What is sex?" with a transcript's context revealing that the patron had no real interest in information, as much as playing around with the service. Many of these goofing-around questions were not problematic in any way.

Rude

The definition for this category was "Patron uses mean phrases or language; is impatient, demanding, or disparaging to the librarian without using offensive language." Examples include: "you know, you're not very smart compared to the person I talked to last..." and "i already have this information can you do any BETTER" [sic].

Offensive Language or Behavior

This category was defined as "Patron uses inappropriate language, including swear words, sexual references, or suggested inappropriate acts." Examples of this category are left to the reader's imagination, with the caveat that, in general, it is not always easy to determine whether something is offensive or inappropriate.

QA&E chose to analyze the transactions of one week. Weeks were chosen from the first and second years of service in order to address (R2), to determine the extent to which inappropriateness has changed as the service has grown. October was selected as an ideal month because it would include heavy use of the service by students.

Attempts wherein no connection was ever made between librarian and patron were eliminated, as were transactions for the training of new staff and Spanish-language transactions (due to a lack of Spanish speakers on the Committee). The resulting 1,369 transactions were categorized and analyzed, 497 from year one and 872 from year two.

Seven subcommittee members were each assigned a range of transcripts to review. Coding results were forwarded to the QA&E co-chairs and the Ask-Colorado project coordinator, who then reviewed all transcripts, standardizing the coding of those marked other than appropriate. Each of the 89 inappropriate transactions was reviewed by the trio, and consensus was achieved for the classification of each transaction. This step was done in effort to maintain the consistency of how the inappropriate behaviors were classed.

Results

General
One of the study's first discoveries was a sharp realization that defining and categorizing human behavior in an online environment is rife with subjectivity. Using two layers of analysis helped objectify categories to some degree, but it is worth noting that inappropriateness is perceived differently by all librarians. Establishing guidelines and operational definitions for such studies is necessary, but it is not likely, and probably not desirable, that all subjectivity be removed from the process. Indeed, perhaps the most valuable lesson learned by QA&E is the importance of assisting virtual librarians in becoming aware of their personal conceptions of appropriate and inappropriate, and how these definitions might differ from those held by their patrons. This awareness is one of the most valuable methods of training in regards to handling "problem" behavior. However, as a matter of comparison and investigation, the transcripts were analyzed and quantified with the following results.

Of the 1,369 analyzed transactions, 89 (6.50 percent) were found to be inappropriate in some manner. Thirty-five (2.56 percent) were categorized "goofing around," 42 (3.07 percent) were "rude," and a total of 12 (0.88 percent) transactions were categorized as "offensive." Results from year one and year two were different. Of the 497 transactions analyzed for year one, a total of 43 (8.65 percent) were inappropriate in some manner. Seventeen were "goofing around," 19 were "rude," and 7 were "offensive" (3.42 percent, 3.82 percent, and 1.41 percent, respectively). The year two gross numbers of inappropriate calls were very similar, but from a much larger sample size (see Figure 7-1).

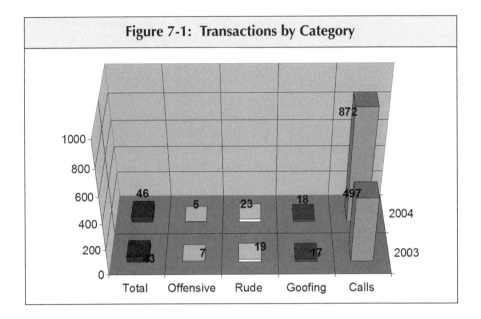

Figure 7-1: Transactions by Category

In summary, inappropriate use was low in year one and still lower in year two. It seems reasonable to assume that inappropriate behavior is not substantially more prevalent in virtual reference than in any other type of reference. It is also notable that only 12 of 89 transactions were categorized as the most severe, "offensive," and thus it seems most inappropriateness is of a less severe nature.

Results of (R1)

While at first blush inappropriate transaction analysis seems to prove that virtual reference services from different states have similar results, a closer look suggests that such a conclusion is not so easy to make (see Figure 7-2). Indeed, all three services show more than 90 percent appropriate use; however, QandANJ, as a precursor to the other studies, does not include the "rude" category, so it is hard to determine whether its results are truly like the other services. Using a chi-squared test of independence [sum of (observed-expected)^2/expected] to compare the relationship between AskColorado and Maryland's AskUsNow!, it is calculated that χ^2 equals 13.107 at p=.01, df=3. This statistically significant result means that the proportions of behaviors differ depending on the population; a pattern in one sample does not accurately predict the patterns in another sample. Hence, when statistical analysis is used to compare the two populations, the populations do not correlate as expected. The discrepancy in analysis results between the two services is most evident in the offensive language category. While AskColorado found 12 of 1,369 transactions to be offensive language, Maryland's AskUsNow! found 23 of 899 transactions to be offensive—almost three times as many as AskColorado.

Figure 7-2: Transaction Analysis by Virtual Reference Service

	AskColorado	QandANJ	Maryland's AskUsNow!
Calls Reviewed	1369	509	899
Appropriate	1280	500	815
Goofing Around	35	7	34
Rude to Librarian	42	n/a	27
Offensive Language, etc.	12	2	23
Total Inappropriate	89	9	84
% Appropriate	93.50%	98.23%	90.66%
% Goofing	2.56%	1.38%	3.78%
% Rude	3.07%	n/a	3.00%
% Offensive	0.88%	0.39%	2.56%
% Inappropriate	6.50%	1.77%	6.01%

Ostensibly, this comparison shows that the central finding of each study—namely, that the vast majority of users of such services use them appropriately—is corroborated, although specifics are harder to generalize. Possible reasons for this include the dynamic nature of online social interaction, the lack of random sampling in each study, and the possible inconsistency among the studies' categorical definitions—itself a result of the subjective nature of inappropriateness.

Results of (R2)

In addressing the question "Has inappropriate behavior on AskColorado changed as the service has evolved?" it became strikingly obvious that it had. The rates of all three categories decreased—goofing around by 1.36 percent, rude by 1.19 percent, offensive by 0.84 percent, and total inappropriateness by 3.38 percent. Essentially, the likelihood of finding an inappropriate transcript was 60 percent smaller in year two as it was in year one.

Speculation on the reason for such a notable decrease is the notion that, as the service evolved, it also matured, resulting in both librarians and patrons with a clearer understanding of what to expect and how to behave in a reference chat environment. Not only is inappropriate use in these studies low, but the AskColorado study demonstrates a decline in such use.

Figure 7-3: Observed and Expected Transaction Behaviors

	Appropriate observed	Appropriate expected	Goofing around observed	Goofing around expected	Rude observed	Rude Expected	Offensive Language observed	Offensive Language expected	Total Observed
AskColorado	1280	1264.57	35	41.65	42	41.65	12	21.13	1369
Maryland's AskUsNow	815	830.43	34	27.35	27	27.35	23	13.87	899

Expected behaviors are calculated as a proportion of the total observed population [for example: appropriate expected = total appropriate expected (2095) * total observed for AskColorado (1369)/total observed for both services (2268) = 1264.57]. The chi-squared test of independence statistic [sum of (observed - expected)/expected] equals 13.107, which is significant at p=.01, df=3.

Results of (R3)

Various patterns of inappropriate use were sought, including analysis by time of day, day of week, interest level, referring Web site, county, and others. Of the patterns examined, three provided some insight: Inappropriate use by time of day, inappropriate use by interest level, and legitimate questions that included some inappropriateness.

Time of day showed a spike during the afternoon, specifically between 2 p.m. and 3 p.m. (see Figure 7-4). The most readily made conclusion about this pattern is that during school hours, some students use the service inappropriately, but this is not a verifiable inference.

Inappropriate use by interest level was difficult to determine conclusively, because patrons self-select one of the following queues: General, K–8, 9–12, College Research, or Professional. Based on these patron selections, K–12 patrons were identified as the population responsible for the majority of inappropriate use, some 63 percent (see Figure 7-5). This percentage is larger than the population's use of the service generally (51 percent for the first year), so it is noteworthy.

While time of day and interest level are, to some degree, revealing and perhaps suggest at least hypothetically that K–12 students are the most likely perpetrators of inappropriate use, the data is not given to generalization and does not seem serious enough to merit targeting K–12 patrons in an attempt to rectify inappropriate use. The fact remains that frequency of such behavior is very low, which is a more important conclusion to be drawn.

Perhaps of greatest interest in regard to patterns was the analysis of the inappropriate transactions that actually included a legitimate reference question. A substantial majority—73 percent—of all inappropriate transactions began with legitimate questions. Broken down by type of inappropriateness, all three showed a substantial majority of them beginning with legitimate use (see Figure 7-6).

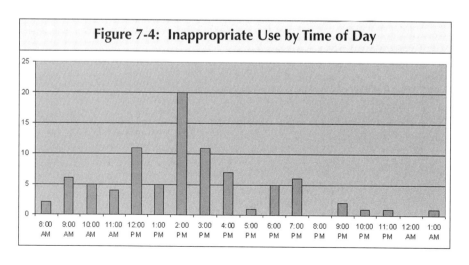

Figure 7-4: Inappropriate Use by Time of Day

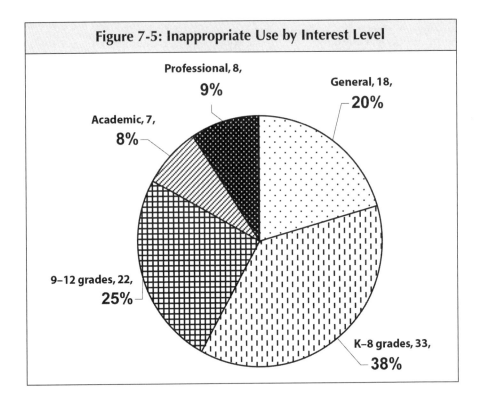

Figure 7-5: Inappropriate Use by Interest Level

Based on this data it can be concluded that the impetus to use the service is appropriate more often than not, but some inappropriateness surfaces during the course of a transaction. Frustration, impatience, unrealistic expectations, and boundary-testing are all possible motivating factors, but this study does not reveal such motivations.

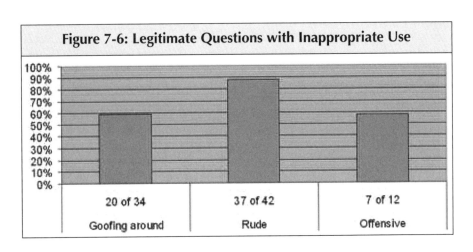

Figure 7-6: Legitimate Questions with Inappropriate Use

Conclusion

Perhaps the most valuable aspect of this study was that it disproved a common myth regarding virtual reference services, namely that they are abused heavily. While comparisons to physical libraries are not easily made, it is reasonable to assume that inappropriate behavior in virtual library transactions, at least as they have matured, is no more likely than at the reference desk of any library. Frequency of inappropriate use is low and may be declining over time. Most inappropriateness is of a less severe nature and originates from legitimate information needs. Inappropriateness in an online environment may be more memorable, and further investigation is warranted in that regard. Such data is valuable in both the promotion of virtual reference services and in the training of their staff members.

In addition to combating myths, the data for this study can be used to illustrate two concepts to virtual reference librarians: 1) inappropriateness is subjective and can often be overcome through mutual understanding of what is expected of people in different behavioral contexts; and 2) virtual reference services and how people behave within their structure are changing as quickly as the technology used to provide them. The limited prevalence and severity of inappropriate behavior in virtual reference services provides evidence that VR is a successful service indeed. It is left to hope that, as technology and behavior continue to evolve, librarians and patrons will learn their nuances and potential.

References

Blessinger, Kelly D. 2002. "Problem Patrons: All Shapes and Sizes." *The Reference Librarian* 36, no. 75: 3–10.

Bobrowsky, Tammy, Lynne Beck, and Malaika Grant. 2005. "The Chat Reference Interview: Practicalities and Advice." *The Reference Librarian* 39, no. 89: 179–191.

Borin, Jacqueline. 2002. "E-Problems, E-Solutions: Electronic Reference and the Problem Patron in the Academic Library." *The Reference Librarian* 36, no. 75:149–161.

Bromberg, Peter. "[DIG_REF] Addressing Pranks (was 'e-mail Ref along with Virtual Ref')." E-mail to DigRef listserve (July 27, 2004). Available: http://finance.groups.yahoo.com/group/dig_ref/message/ 9501

Bullard, Sharon W. 2002. "Gypsies, Tramps and Rage: Coping with Difficult Patrons." *The Reference Librarian* 36, no. 75: 245–252.

Chattoo, Calmer D. 2002. "The Problem Patron: Is There One in Your Library?" *The Reference Librarian* 36, no. 75: 11–22.

Chelton, Mary K. 2002. "The 'Problem Patron' Public Libraries Created." *The Reference Librarian* 36, no. 75: 23–32.

Currie, C. L. 2002. "Difficult Library Patrons in Academe: It's All in the Eye of the Beholder." *The Reference Librarian* 36, no. 75: 45–54.

Jensen, J. D. 2004. "It's the Information Age, so Where's the Information? Why Our Students Can't Find It and What We Can Do to Help." *College Teaching* 52, no. 3: 107–112.

Kwon, Nahyun. 2004. "Assessing the Virtual Reference Success Using the Revised RUSA Guidelines for Behavioral Performance of Reference and Information Service Providers." *Online Proceedings of the 6th Annual Virtual Reference Desk Conference*. Available: www.vrd2004.org/proceedings/presentation.cfm?PID=396

Lee, Ian J. 2004. "Do Virtual Reference Librarians Dream of Digital Reference Questions?: A Qualitative and Quantitative Analysis of E-mail and Chat Reference." *Australian Academic & Research Libraries* 35, no. 2: 95–110.

Peatling, Gary K. 2002. "Historical Perspective on Problem Patrons from the British Public Library Sector, 1850–1919." *The Reference Librarian* 36, no. 75: 33–43.

Radford, Marie. 2003. "In Synch? Evaluating Chat Reference Transcripts." *Online Proceedings of the 5th Annual Virtual Reference Desk Conference.* Available: www.vrd2003.org/proceedings/ presentation.cfm?PID=231

Radford, Marie, and Joseph Thompson. 2004. "Yo Dude! Y R U Typin So Slow? Interpersonal Communication in Chat Reference." *Online Proceedings of the 6th Annual Virtual Reference Desk Conference.* Available: www.vrd2004.org/proceedings/presentation. cfm?PID=325

Smyth, Joanne. 2003. "Virtual Reference Transcript Analysis: A Few Models." *Searcher* 11, no. 3: 26–30.

Taylor, Daniel, and George S. Porter. 2002. "The Problem Patron and the Academic Library Web Site as Virtual Reference Desk." *The Reference Librarian* 36, no. 75: 163–172.

Tennant, Roy. 2003. "Revisiting Digital Reference." *Library Journal* 128, no. 1: 38–40.

Thompson, Joseph. "Re: [DIG_REF] To Block or Not to Block: Belligerent IM Patrons." E-mail to DigRef listserve (March 24, 2005). Available: http://finance. groups.yahoo.com/group/dig_ref/message/ 10938

Ward, David. 2003. "Using Virtual Reference Transcripts for Staff Training." *Reference Services Review* 31, no. 1: 46–56.

Part IV

Pulling It Together:
VR Training

Meeting the Challenges of Reference Service in a Hybrid Environment: Teaching LIS Students Today

Debbie L. Rabina

Overview

General reference training at most library schools still focuses primarily on the print sources, proprietary databases, and face-to-face encounters of traditional reference service. The increasing demand for virtual reference requires educators to revise training to accommodate the practical and theoretical capabilities of students who are interested in careers as reference librarians.

Here are the findings of a preliminary study of how library and information science (LIS) students are prepared to provide reference services in a hybrid environment. Forty-two library school students in a general reference course at Pratt Institute were split into two sections, each with a different curriculum. The curriculums differed in theoretical emphasis, suggested and required sources, and assignments. Students were assessed to determine if the different training approaches impacted their skill in providing virtual and face-to-face reference.

The author makes suggestions for a theoretical and methodological approach to training LIS students for work in a hybrid reference environment.

Introduction and Background

Students in library and information schools preparing for careers as reference providers will, in many cases, find themselves providing reference services in a hybrid environment, catering to patrons in face-to-face and virtual and chat reference settings. Reference services are defined as "all the functions performed by a trained librarian ... (in person, by telephone, or electronically), including ... instructing users in the selection and use of appropriate tools and techniques for finding information, conducting searches on behalf of the patron, directing users to the location of library resources, assisting in the evaluation of information, referring patrons to resources outside the library when appropriate." (ODLIS, 2005) Digital reference is defined as "reference services requested and provided over the Internet ... or Web-based submission forms, usually answered by librarians in the reference department of a library, sometimes by the participants in a collaborative reference system serving more than one institution" (ODLIS, 2005).

Digital, or virtual, reference is a tool, a means of communication. It is considered a subset of traditional reference services, and all tenets of traditional reference—for example, answering questions, aiding in selection, conducting research, and evaluating information—apply to it as well. In terms of training reference librarians, this means that, in addition to all the skills for traditional reference services, such as knowing reference sources, meeting information needs, instructing patrons, conducting searches, and evaluating information, they need to be taught the skills for digital reference.

Purpose of Study

Based on data collected in two reference sections of a course taught at Pratt Institute in New York City, this chapter provides suggestions for training library school students to work in a hybrid reference environment. The goal is to present a curriculum that covers all areas of reference work, traditional and virtual, balancing both reference services and resources while providing as many simulated real-life situations as possible.

More specifically, the researcher set out to examine how various aspects of virtual and chat reference could be incorporated into a curriculum in a way that made them not simply appended but integral to the course work. Not unlike the study by Janes and Hill (2002), this too was an exploratory study, with an emphasis on framework development and future investigation. The hope was that this study would establish the groundwork for a large-scale examination of effective ways to incorporate virtual and chat reference training into a standard general reference course and, by focusing on digital reference services, contribute to the development of a digital reference agenda, as outlined by Lankes (2005).

Library educators who teach reference courses devote much time to preparing the curriculum. Since reference works are frequently updated, there is a constant need to select current textbooks to match the institution's library holdings. In addition to keeping apace with new sources and other developments, teaching reference requires frequent library visits and regular reading of the literature. In recent years, reference educators have faced the challenge of integrating virtual and chat reference training into the general reference course curriculum. This integration is necessary to prepare students to enter the hybrid service systems they will encounter after graduating, and fulfills the requirements of many general course descriptions.

Literature Review

Research in reference education addresses the question of reference education in general and training for virtual and chat reference in particular, but none of the research specifically focuses on providing virtual reference service training to incoming professionals—students in LIS schools—within the framework of the general reference core curriculum. Most of the literature focuses on reference training in general (Bawden, Vilar and Zabukovec, 2004; Chandler, 2001; Daniel and Lazinger, 1998; Kajberg and Lørrig, 2005) and on methods of training working professionals to provide virtual reference services (Hirko and Ross, 2004; Ronan, 2003; Smith, 2002). Essential virtual reference service skills that are emphasized pertain more to information technology proficiency (working with multiple browsers and keyboarding proficiency) and less to unique search strategies and sources appropriate for virtual reference (Lipow, 2003; Meola and Stormont, 2002; Ronan, 2003).

Reference instruction is an important part of the LIS curriculum, and its content and relevance are examined and reevaluated regularly. Curriculums in LIS schools have been studied by several researchers in the past few years. Perhaps the most comprehensive of these studies is a white paper prepared by Smith presenting an overview of reference training and focusing on emerging virtual reference (Smith, 2002). Smith, along with other researchers, identified a list of core competencies for digital reference education (DREI, 2004). More detailed training guidelines for virtual reference are found in a book by Hirko and Ross (2004). They outline a complete training program designed to prepare reference librarians for work in a hybrid reference environment.

General reference remains part of the core curriculum in most LIS programs in the United States. International standards, such as those drafted by the International Federation of Library Associations and Institutions (*Standards for Library Schools*) (Daniel and Lazinger, 1998) and studied by Kajberg and Lørrig (2005), have also identified reference as a core competency, one with particular importance in a multicultural environment. Studies that focused on core competencies outside the United States have also singled out reference as a key component (Bawden et al., 2004). Several researchers have reaffirmed the need to continue training reference librarians, arguing that they are more important than ever with the demand for their services growing. Chandler (2001) provides statistics from various sources to demonstrate past and projected growth in reference positions. Curriculums in general reference also have been the subject of several studies in recent years, examining both historical and current aspects and making recommendations for the future.

However, a number of changes have been observed over the years. Central to these has been a shift in emphasis from reference titles to reference services. Powell and Raber (1994) found that, though there has been a gradual shift toward greater interest in services, individual reference titles are still critical to general reference training, and educators use them in conjunction with technology-based services.

These conclusions have been echoed by other authors who consider the new roles of reference and the development of new reference curriculums. Like Powell and Raber (1994), other researchers have examined the ways technology has affected reference services. Chandler (2001) emphasizes the need for more technology skills on the part of reference librarians, as well as a better understanding of information-seeking behavior. According to Wilson (2000), training users to access and evaluate information sources is central to reference work. To support his view, he chose to break up the teaching of the reference course at the University of North Texas.

Another important role for the reference librarian is undergraduate instruction. A recent study by Burke (2005) found that an instructional program for undergraduates at the University of Albany increased reference statistics, demonstrating that bibliographic instruction not only improved the search skills of undergraduate students but also increased their use of reference services.

With regard to teaching methods, Powell and Raber (1994) demonstrated that reference instructors use a wide range of teaching methods including lecture, discussion, self-guidance, case study, and teamwork. Costello, Lenholt and Stryker (2004: 453) warned against lecturing in the classroom: "Lecture is an especially ineffective instructional technique for Gen Y students because these students prefer active, or kinesthetic, learning environments."

Teaching Reference: A Personal Perspective

Reference instructors spend a great deal of time considering what to include and what not to include in a reference course. Personal experience indicates that it is easier to add elements to a course than to take them out. The result is a continual growth of course material. This includes more print titles and electronic sources, greater emphasis on evaluation, and an increasing focus on reference processes, such as the reference interview, information-seeking behavior, and reader advisory. In addition to the tools currently used in libraries, there remains a need to study classic reference tools that are significant milestones in the development of reference. Newly degreed librarians should be familiar with these classics, because they are part of the development of reference and the basis for many existing reference tools. An additional advantage of introducing students to classic references is that they provide a graphic example of the structure of reference tools in a way that is not always obvious when looking at an online source. For example, the 800 volumes of the New York Public Library print catalog is an example of a dictionary catalog that is also of worth because it includes rare titles that are still not included in the online catalog. Other classics that are part of the reference heritage include the *National Union Catalog Pre-1956 Imprints*, Balay's *Guide to Reference Books*, the ninth edition of *Encyclopædia Britannica*, and Bartlett's *Familiar Quotations*.

The content of a course is usually dictated by course description and goals, as given in the departmental course listing, and by the personal input, interpretation, and world view of the instructor. The course that was the basis for this study, generically referred to as general reference and specifically called "Information Services and Sources," is described in the course catalog as follows:

Covers reference in real and virtual environments. The course introduces the selection and evaluation of resources in all formats, the development of searching techniques, strategies for user-centered service, matching user needs to resources, and the provision of information services in changing technological environments. (Rabina, 2007)

Broken down into its elements, this description translates into the following classes and requirements: Classes devoted to familiarizing students with resources, classes devoted to selecting and evaluating those resources, classes devoted to understanding user needs, and classes devoted to providing resources and services equally in real and virtual environments.

Reference courses change frequently, and rarely are two courses taught the same way from one semester to the next. Course changes are necessitated by the evolving reference environment and skills LIS students bring to the course.

Participating in the study were 42 students divided into two sections of young, computer-literate individuals. The majority (67 percent) had a recent college degree, from 2000 or later, so that it was likely their academic experience included OPACs and online resources. Since most of the students had backgrounds in the humanities and social sciences (83 percent) and experience working in libraries (60 percent), the group as a whole had a good set of skills and knowledge.

Today's students—those with and without professional library experience—arrive at LIS schools with an advanced and often self-acquired set of searching skills. While they may lack the professional terminology to describe what it is they are doing, they often are able to find answers to ready reference questions with the same speed, skill, and level of ability as a trained librarian. Their use of the Internet is regular, ongoing, and quite sophisticated. It is part of their daily lives. As a course assignment, students were asked for a bibliographic essay describing all the information sources they used daily, and the list was quite impressive. Students are socially, politically, and professionally aware. They have little use for traditional reference assignments based on the "treasure hunt" model. They can complete such assignments faster than instructors can write them. How then, does one think of reference in the age of Google? Not surprisingly, the library has changed from the place where one goes to "look it up" to the place where one goes when all looking has failed. It has become the venue of last resort. Face-to-face reference work is associated less with ready reference and much more with research assistance, bibliographic instruction, and literacy training. On the other hand, virtual and chat reference occupies a growing place in the professional literature, at conferences, and in scholarly communication. By nature, chat reference seems more suited for a ready reference agenda. Therefore, how can chat reference be integrated into a course curriculum that is increasingly service- and research-based?

That was the challenge the researcher faced when teaching general reference. Scheduling conditions necessitated that the researcher teach two sections of a general reference course during the same semester, and this was taken as an opportunity to design an experiment that would attempt to identify optimal ways of teaching reference while training students to work in a hybrid environment.

Prior to that, virtual reference did not receive much attention in the course curriculum. One session out of 15 was devoted to the topic, and that session included a demo of chat reference from a user perspective, some readings, and a class discussion of differences between working virtual, chat, and face-to-face reference. Given the emphasis virtual reference had in the official course description and in scholarly discourse, it was worth more than 1/15—a mere 6.6 percent—of the course content, that is, more than a single class devoted to a short history of virtual reference with a one-hour demo, which, as previous experience had shown, was bound to run into technical difficulties.

Two alternative curriculums were developed, one for each section, and tested simultaneously. The first curriculum was geared to training students to work in a very fast-paced reference environment, with an emphasis on virtual reference, ready reference, and speedy delivery. The second curriculum emphasized a research environment and focused on anchoring reference in a context of explorative learning and scholarly communication. Neither curriculum compromised any of the required skills all reference students should learn. Although each curriculum had its own goals, neither was a pure type. Each reflected the course description and objectives provided in the course catalog. Digital reference—specifically chat reference—was integrated into both courses and introduced as a tool, a service, and a method of delivery, all at once.

The two curriculums were designed to test two somewhat contradictory assumptions. The first was that, due to the inherent nature of chat reference, students training to work in chat reference should receive more instruction in answering ready reference questions in a limited time frame. The second assumption was that, as a result of the decline of foot traffic in libraries, reference services focus more on instruction and research assistance, and training should emphasize these processes.

The first curriculum was designed to be fast-paced. Students were instructed in various ways of maximizing Web searches by using a variety of search engines, particularly Google Scholar, Vivísimo, and Teoma (which has since merged with Ask.com). The students spent time comparing and evaluating the results from the different search engines and then applying rigorous measures to compare the results with those from proprietary reference tools and print sources. Once they completed the assigned reference process, they were asked to present the same problem to a virtual reference service and to a face-to-face service and compare their own results to those of the professionals with respect to speed, comprehensiveness, and depth of answer.

The second curriculum, with its strong emphasis on research, required that students make use of all reference venues to explore a particular topic. Students were assigned a single research topic for the duration of the semester—Fabergé eggs. This topic was chosen because (1) it was general enough to be included in tools used by the generalist at the reference desk; (2) it was flexible enough so it could be expanded and narrowed, as necessary, in order to be researched in various tools, from indexes to directories; and (3) it was related to art, which is very much a focus at Pratt Institute. Students were to search this topic using various reference formats: print, Internet, and proprietary bibliographies; indexes; directories; and others. Once they completed searching their sources, they were asked to present the same question to a virtual reference service, for example: "I am writing a paper about Fabergé eggs. I am interested in sales information about other decorative *objets d'art* of the same period. I want to know how much they sold for and any other available information, such as who sold them, who bought them, and where they were sold."

The objective of this exercise was to examine the reasoning behind the second assumption: While there is still room to teach students how to enhance and maximize their Internet search skills, there seems to be little need for comprehensive training in the area, since students come to LIS programs with a solid background in Internet searching. The tools and processes associated with ready reference are now in the public domain, and ready reference does not necessarily require professional training—practically anyone can do it. Therefore, the focus of reference education must be on what is necessary for both students and users. Since libraries have the advantage over other entities in providing in-depth comprehensive research assistance, direct reference education should be directed toward the research process. Hence virtual reference: The new service of choice at many academic and public libraries. How to incorporate this new service into the research process?

Observed Outcomes

While this study was driven by suggestions that were tested, the experiment served primarily as a pilot project to help formulate a hypothesis that could be further tested in followup research. The results from both class sections are based on the researcher's observations and on a questionnaire completed by each student. Working with virtual reference in a classroom presented problems in technology, logistics, and ethics. The technical problems were frustrating. Live services often did not work properly: Students were thrown out of chats when computer screens froze; wireless network connections sometimes failed; libraries did not actually have the service available at the posted hours; and students working with Macintosh computers (35 percent) were not able to view Web pages on-screen. Only about 50 percent of in-class attempts to conduct virtual and chat reference transactions were successful. Students working at home had a higher success rate—about 65 to 70 percent upon first attempt.

The logistical problems were related to finding appropriate libraries for chat reference interactions. Both sections met in the evening, a time when many area public libraries do not provide chat reference services. The New York Public Library, for example, provides chat service only until 5 p.m., and the Brooklyn Public Library does not offer any chat reference service except for ready reference homework help.

Finally, there arose the ethical question of whether it was justified to use libraries nationwide for the purpose of reference training. While it was relatively simple to contact any number of libraries, requiring only a zip code as proof of residency, was it morally justified to do so? It appeared that students were not troubled by this aspect. Only 18 percent had ethical reservations about taking up chat reference services outside their library system.

When planning the two curriculums, the expectation was that by semester's end, each group would have sufficient virtual reference experience to analyze, much in the same way they evaluate their experiences using a particular online bibliography or print encyclopedia. But as a result of the technical, logistical, and ethical problems described above, the students received only sketchy exposure to chat reference—perhaps a little more than in past courses, but certainly not enough to allow them to assess its value as a ready reference or research tool. No significant differences between chat reference and face-to-face reference were reported by students in either section. A considerable number of students preferred their chat reference experience (41 percent) to their face-to-face experience (38 percent), with the remainder showing no preference. A majority of students (76 percent) reported that they would prefer to provide face-to-face reference in professional positions.

From the evidence gathered, it seemed that overall, students in the ready reference section received more accurate responses to their inquiries than did the students in the research section. It was also found that librarians used Google as the first, and many times the only, search method; however, this occurred more frequently in chat reference than in face-to-face reference, where many librarians turned to the OPAC first. When students replicated Google searches in class, they found several ways searches could be improved. Enhancements included constructing more complex search queries; turning to more specialized tools as first, or perhaps second, points of access; and being more selective about Google hits. Students found that using advanced features, such as searching for results within a particular domain using Google advanced search options, improved results. For example, using Google to search for transcripts of President Bush's speeches produced better results than searching the White House Web site directly. Such techniques were not used by librarians. Students in the research section were often asked to leave an e-mail address with a librarian who promised to get back with an answer. This led students to believe that chat reference was more suited to answering ready reference questions than research questions, and that digital reference might be a more suited to answering research questions.

Assessment of student ready reference skills was done near the end of the course with a "reference marathon," in which students were asked to answer ten ready reference questions in one hour. In the first (ready) reference section, students took 25 to 40 minutes to answer the questions, while in the second (research) section, students took 32 to more than 60 minutes. Three students did not complete the assignment within the allotted hour. While both sections received training in answering ready reference questions within specified time limits, the students in the first section received more intensive training than those in the second section. In the first section, 48 percent of the students reported they found the ready reference part of the training helpful for reference work in general, and 65 percent reported they thought it was particularly important for virtual and chat reference settings. This compares with 41 percent and 47 percent, respectively, in the second section. When students in both sections were asked to rank the value of the training they received, the students in the first section reported that the most important process was answering ready reference questions under time constraints, and those in the second section reported that the most important skill was how to assist users writing research papers.

Recommendations for Further Research

This study provided valuable feedback on some of the ways to proceed in the quest to make virtual reference training a valuable experience for LIS students. Given the nature of some of the problems encountered, instruction in chat reference appears to be better suited in a controlled learning environment than in a real-world setting. The latter provides too many challenges to distract students and instructor from the main goal of training students to provide service in chat reference environments. Library educators should team with commercial providers of chat reference services to allow classroom use of the services, so that students can experience chat reference as users and service providers. In addition, from the evidence that was gathered, it appears that general reference courses would benefit most from chat reference using a narrower ready reference approach while continuing to focus primarily on research assistance.

Most librarians observed during the semester used Google as a first, and in many cases single, point of access to the Internet. There seems to be value in teaching students how to enhance online searching by constructing useful queries and by using more targeted tools as a first or second point of access. Although the use of chat reference services for a research-based project was found to be unsuitable within the general reference framework, it might be tried in the future in specialized reference courses. Still, the question of suitability of chat reference for more in-depth reference assistance should be further explored. The increasing reluctance of users to physically patronize libraries is likely to include users at the research level as well, and we should explore ways to serve their information needs. This may be especially useful for individuals at the initial stages of their research career. Chat reference, if it takes hold, has the potential of changing scholarly communication, particularly as it pertains to the researcher's relationship with the library.

Virtual reference is still attracting a great deal of attention and generating interest in research and practice. Libraries are investing in this service to better serve their patrons. Consequently, it is only expected that library schools will continue to search for ways to improve training in this area so that students are better prepared to provide reference services in a hybrid environment.

References

Bawden, David, Polona Vilar, and Vlasta Zabukovec. 2004. "Competencies and Capabilities for the Digital Age." *Online Information*, 2004 Conference Proceedings. Available: www.online-information. co.uk/ol06/conferenceproceedings.html

Burke, Gerald. 2005. "Information Literacy: Bringing a Renaissance to Reference." *Portal: Libraries and the Academy* 5, no. 3: 353–369.

Chandler, Yvonne J. 2001. "Reference in Library and Information Science Education." *Library Trends* 50, no. 2: 245–262.

Costello, Barbara, Robert Lenholt, and Judson Stryker. 2004. "Using Blackboard in Library Instruction: Addressing the Learning Styles of Generations X and Y." *The Journal of Academic Librarianship* 30, no. 6: 452–460.

Daniel, Evelyn, and Susan Lazinger. 1998. "Standards for Library Schools, 1976: Update: A Preliminary Report to the Standing Committee on Education and Training (64th IFLA General Conference, Amsterdam, August 1998)." International Federation of Library Associations and Institutions. Available: www.ifla.org/ IV/ifla65/ papers/085-159e.htm (accessed May 2006).

Hirko, Buff, and Mary Bucher Ross. 2004. *Virtual Reference Training: The Complete Guide to Providing Anytime, Anywhere Answers*. Chicago, IL: American Library Association.

Janes, Joseph, and Chrystie Hill. 2002. "Finger on the Pulse: Librarians Describe Evolving Reference Practice in an Increasingly Digital World." *Reference and User Services Quarterly* 42, no. 1: 54–65.

Kajberg, Leif, and Leif Lørrig, eds. 2005. "European Curriculum Reflections on Library and Information Science Education." The Royal School of Library and Information Science, Denmark. Available: www.kf.vu.lt/site_files_doc/LIS_Bologna.pdf (accessed May 2006).

Lankes, R. David. 2005. "Digital Reference Research: Fusing Research and Practice." *Reference and User Services Quarterly* 44, no. 4: 320–326.

Lipow, Anne Grodzins. 2003. *The Virtual Reference Librarian's Handbook*. New York: Neal-Schuman.

Meola, Marc, and Sam Stormont. 2002. *Starting and Operating Live Virtual Reference Services*. New York: Neal-Schuman.

ODLIS: Online Dictionary for Library and Information Science (October 2005). Available: http://lu.com/odlis/

Powell, Ronald R., and Douglas Raber. 1994. "Education for Reference/Information Service: A Quantitative and Qualitative Analysis of Basic Reference Courses." *The Reference Librarian* 43: 145–172.

Rabina, D. 2007. "LIS652-Section 1: Information Services and Resources." Course Syllabus. Available: www.google.com/url?sa=t&ct=res&ed=1&url=http%3A%2F %2Fpratt.edu%2F~drabina (accessed August 2007).

Ronan, Jana Smith. 2003. *Chat Reference: A Guide to Live Virtual Reference Services*. Westport, CT: Libraries Unlimited.

"Rubric for Digital Reference Service Providers." 2004. DREI: Digital Reference Education Initiative (May 2006). Available: http://drei.syr.edu/pdf/DREICompetencies Draft092004.pdf

Smith, Linda C. 2002. "Education for Digital Reference Service." *White Paper Prepared for the Digital Reference Research Symposium, August 2–3, 2003*. Cambridge, MA: Harvard University. Available: http://leep.lis.uiuc.edu/fall02/lis404lea/drs education.html (accessed October 2005).

Wilson, Myong C. 2000. "Evolution or Entropy? Changing Reference/User Culture and the Future of Reference Librarians." *Reference & User Services Quarterly* 39, no. 4: 387–390.

Chapter 9

A Comprehensive VR Training Program

Joann Wasik

Overview
Recognizing the need for including virtual reference education in existing LIS curricula, the Digital Reference Education Initiative (DREI) was formed to examine the state of virtual reference education and training. DREI sought to bring together the collective experience of reference practitioners, library educators, paraprofessionals, and virtual reference software developers to develop core competencies and educational approaches to virtual reference. The competencies and rubrics outlined in this chapter were the outcome of this collaborative effort.

Introduction and Background
In the past decade, virtual reference services[1] have gone from something of a library novelty to a mainstream service offered by thousands of libraries and other types of organizations. With users quickly adopting the Internet as a popular method of communication, reference librarians recognized the opportunity to deliver information services to their communities in a new, electronic medium. At present, reference transactions by e-mail and Web-based forms are giving way to instant messaging and other means of real-time, synchronous methods. While this technological evolution has sparked new opportunities and capabilities for information provision, it has also created new sets of challenges for reference providers. Increased computer proficiency, multi-tasking skills, and the ability to change and adapt rapidly to new software and technologies are just some of the demands on librarians, most of whom are required to provide reference service at an increasingly "faster, better, cheaper" rate.

While many patrons have been happy to embrace the various online reference services, some reference librarians and staff have been more resistant to

---

[1] Throughout this chapter, "digital reference" and "virtual reference" are used interchangeably to indicate any type of electronic reference transaction.

change. Inadequate computer skills, fear of change, and the resentment of added job duties have all been cited as barriers to staff buy-in to virtual reference tasks (Berube, 2003; Meola and Stormont, 2002; Ronan, 2001). Chat reference in particular, with its faster pace and multiple synchronous patrons, has engendered much fear and loathing among some librarians. Most reference staff, however, become less resistant to virtual reference duties once they have received adequate training and gained more experience (Janes, 2002; Salem, Balraj and Lilly, 2003). Although many of the same skills are used by reference librarians in both face-to-face and virtual reference transactions, working with a remote clientele demands a special set of skills not readily acquired on the job. Administrators have finally recognized that even seasoned staff cannot simply be transplanted from the traditional reference desk to the virtual reference desk and be expected to thrive, but that training must be provided for effective service to occur.

Although continued training is necessary for optimal staff performance, virtual reference training is particularly important for reference librarians who are new to virtual reference or who find providing virtual reference services difficult. Staff training of any kind should be viewed as a necessary component of staff development and not simply a luxury. The goal of such training is, of course, the constant upgrading of staff skills and abilities, and there is no end to it. There will always be new skills to develop. Indeed, in an era of rapid technological change, routine training is critical to providing effective virtual reference services.

The lack of virtual reference training is not restricted to existing librarians and older staff. New and recent LIS graduates, too, often face the daunting prospect of providing virtual reference services with little or no training or experience. Although these graduates are generally comfortable with technology and have used computers since childhood, they often face the same challenges as older staff when confronted with having to provide virtual reference services. The integration of virtual reference into traditional reference duties is frequently reflected in job advertisements for library positions: Virtual reference experience is often stated as a requirement for reference librarian positions. Yet despite the demand for applicants with virtual reference experience, most library and information schools still do not feature virtual reference in their curricula.

As of this writing, over 50 percent of Master's-level library and information science programs accredited by the American Library Association (ALA) do not address virtual reference in their reference courses. Moreover, less than half of the programs that do discuss virtual reference do so exclusively through readings (Philbrick and Cleveland, 2006). The need for the inclusion of virtual reference education into the existing LIS curricula has been recognized by many educators and practitioners, and this topic was the subject of much discussion at the 4th Annual VRD Conference in Chicago, Illinois, in 2002. As a result, the Digital Reference Education Initiative (DREI), funded by the Institute of Museum and Library Services and overseen by the Information Institute of Syracuse, was formed to examine the state of virtual reference education and training. DREI sought to bring together the collective experience of reference practitioners, library educators, paraprofessionals, and virtual reference software developers to develop core competencies and educational approaches to virtual reference. The resulting competencies and rubrics outlined in this book have been developed by the collaborative effort of the DREI Board (see Figure 9-1).

This workbook is geared to LIS instructors who want to incorporate virtual reference practices in their curricula, existing reference practitioners who want to initiate or upgrade their virtual reference training methods, and those who are interested in virtual reference competencies and training.

The Three Levels of Competency

This section examines the idea of establishing core competencies for virtual reference for both reference practitioners and LIS students. These competencies have been identified as the skills and expertise that reference staff must demonstrate in order to provide effective virtual reference service.

The core competencies detailed in this book focus on teaching virtual reference at three different levels, starting with basic skills and progressing to higher level skills as student and/or staff proficiency increases. It is important to note that these three levels are viewed as a progression, with the Intermediate skills building upon the Basic skills, and the Advanced skills building on both the Beginning and Intermediate skills.

The *Beginning level* focuses on skills that are needed to perform reference tasks at the basic or most fundamental level required for the position. At this level, reference students and practitioners demonstrate a basic understanding of the major concepts related to virtual reference, such as the structure of the service, its functions, and its impact on other departments and/or institutions. The Beginning level is also characterized by the ability to reflect on the service's processes, but is somewhat limited in scope.

The *Intermediate level* has a conceptual focus. In addition to performing tasks at a level appropriate for the position, the student or practitioner also

Figure 9-1: DREI Board Members

June Abbas	Lydia Harris	Lorri Mon
Matthew Bejune	Maurita Holland	Jeff Pomerantz
Blythe Bennett	Nancy Huling	Marie Radford
Donna Dinberg	Joseph Janes	Linda C. Smith
Connie Van Fleet	Kathleen Kern	Joann Wasik
Franceen Gaudet	David Lankes	
Abby Goodrum	Ken Lavender	

has a deeper level of understanding about why, when, and how these tasks are performed. This level is characterized by an increased understanding of the salient processes and applications of virtual reference and its related tasks, as well as the inherent relationships between the tasks and personnel that such services create.

The *Advanced level* features an administrative focus in which higher-level skills and the ability to think critically about the virtual reference service and its performance have developed. At the Advanced level, LIS students and reference practitioners are able to demonstrate a much greater breadth of knowledge about various components of virtual reference service than at previous levels. The Advanced level is characterized by a greater ability to objectively collect, synthesize, and evaluate information relating to the service and its staff. As reference staff progress through the competencies and achieve the Advanced level, their expanded knowledge and flexibility become increasingly beneficial to both their virtual reference service and to their institutions.

Since virtual reference has been incorporated into traditional face-to-face reference work in many libraries, students enrolled in graduate LIS programs should be versed in virtual reference practices in order to be competitive in the job market after graduation. As a result, it is highly desirable that all MLIS students achieve the Advanced level of the competencies by the completion of their graduate reference coursework. It is the responsibility of both reference educators and accredited MLIS graduate programs to prepare their graduates to enter the job market with the best possible set of skills. Students interested in reference work, then, can best be prepared by their achieving such core competencies as those outlined in this chapter.

Some libraries may not see the need for all staff to progress to the Advanced level. In libraries that practice a tiered model of reference service, for example, it may be adequate for some staff members' performance to remain at the Beginning or Intermediate levels. Tiered reference service is a practice where paraprofessional staff or graduate students offer frontline support for repetitive and directional questions, with more difficult questions answered by reference librarians (Massey-Burzio, 1992). Yet for most libraries, a comprehensive training program to upgrade the skills of all reference practitioners to the Advanced Level is preferred.

Training and Education

This section outlines topics related to the creation, implementation, and managing of training programs and materials for virtual reference.

The fundamental goal of every reference department is to provide high-quality information at a consistent level of service. To achieve such a goal, regular training must occur in order for staff to upgrade and refine their skills. While most organizations conduct training sessions when a new product or service is introduced, many libraries make the mistake of viewing training as an isolated event, an activity initiated to address a particular need at a specific moment. This "Band-Aid" approach to training may suffice for the short term, but inevitably, staff skills erode without regular training in the face of changing technology and information resources. Expense and lack of time are often viewed as barriers to ongoing training, but training programs and materials should evolve over time to address staff and user needs. While there is often a cost incurred in creating and conducting a training program (in time, money, or both), the investment is likely to be repaid quickly through greater staff capabilities and more effective service.

LIS educators face similar challenges in providing their reference students with adequate virtual reference training. With courses already brimming with readings, assignments, and reference activities, many LIS instructors are hard-pressed to create adequate time for student virtual reference training as well. Despite such challenges, though, it is recommended that LIS students receive some virtual reference training in order to be competitive in the reference job market after graduation. As a result, LIS students would greatly benefit by having a solid conceptual understanding of and some hands-on experience with virtual reference by the time they graduate from their MLIS programs. Such training could be incorporated into the existing reference curriculum or offered in a separate core or advanced reference class on virtual reference. Partnerships with the reference departments at LIS schools' libraries may provide an avenue to some virtual reference training opportunities, as well as volunteer opportunities at other information organizations (e.g., the Internet Public Library).

Importance of Virtual Reference Training and Education

Training is an organization's investment in its workforce. Its value, however, is frequently underestimated by administrators and staff alike, who often dislike the cost involved or the time taken away from regular tasks. Training programs are sometimes initiated as a response to a specific problem or set of difficulties for which no plan has been previously instituted. While any training is better than no training, such "reactionary" training is certainly less effective than a training program that has been planned and developed in advance. Successful training programs require a great deal of planning and preparation prior to implementation and must originate from the service's administrators. It is essential that administrators take a proactive stance on training for their staff and avoid relying on crisis "management" techniques to initiate a training program in reaction to problems. With proper training, reference staff are also better equipped to cope with constant technology changes and increased user demands. Upon completion of a successful training and education program, LIS students and reference staff alike can offer improved skills, exhibit greater confidence in their abilities, and demonstrate increased motivation.

Exposure to virtual reference issues and hands-on experience for LIS students offers other benefits as well. The inclusion of actual virtual reference practice sessions allows students and educators alike to evaluate how well the students have absorbed the conceptual material taught in class. Students put into practice what they have studied in class and gain a real-world perspective in reference work while still in school. Such practical experience is critical to students' cognitive and affective understanding of virtual reference, and their problem-solving skills can be refined in a supportive environment. The benefits of hands-on virtual reference experience for students extend to LIS faculty as well. In addition to preparing their students for reference work post-graduation, educators stay current with the latest technology and topics related to virtual reference. Based on student performance and feedback regarding their virtual reference experiences, educators can revise and adapt their teaching materials, exercises, and techniques more effectively to meet student needs and enhance curricular goals and objectives. The process also presents LIS educators with increased opportunities to enhance their own research and scholarship endeavors, as they observe student practices and the challenges that actual virtual reference transactions present.

Training generally occurs in stages, as reference staff and LIS students alike possess varying levels of education and experience and thus must first achieve basic skills upon which to build more highly developed skills. Libraries seeking to upgrade the skills of their reference practitioners can schedule a series of training programs based on desired skill level, while LIS courses may offer Beginning level virtual reference practices in a core reference course and Intermediate and Advanced level instruction in higher-level courses.

The benefits of training in general have been well noted. McNamara (1999) lists the following as some of the general benefits of staff training:

- increased job satisfaction and morale
- increased motivation
- increased efficiencies in processes
- increased capacity to adopt new technologies and methods
- increased innovation in strategies and products
- reduced employee turnover

All of these benefits certainly apply to personnel staffing virtual reference services. A well-trained staff can make discernable improvements to the service, including its reliability, efficiency, and accuracy. Additionally, all these factors help reduce the costs associated with providing the service—an important feature in this era of flat and reduced operating budgets. For LIS students, virtual reference training not only allows them to compete for available reference positions, but also to contribute to their organizations much more quickly. Students with virtual reference experience face a flatter learning curve and are able to take on more complex tasks sooner than their peers who lack such training and experience.

Who Receives Training?

To operate on an optimal level, all reference staff—paraprofessionals and MLIS-degreed librarians alike—should receive some amount of virtual reference training. In most organizations, training programs are created for reference librarians or experts who actively respond to user inquiries and the staff members who support them in the operation of the overall service (Lankes and Kasowitz, 1998). It is recommended here that even those reference staff members who may not directly provide virtual reference services should receive virtual reference training at least through the Beginning level, if only to gain an understanding of the service's policies, goals, and procedures. In response to declining budgets and staff cuts, many libraries have instituted employee cross-training programs, in which staff from one department are trained in various tasks in a different department. Having all reference staff members achieve at least the Beginning level of competency as outlined in the DREI rubrics, whether they actually provide remote reference service or not, helps ensure that service policies, procedures, and operations are understood by all staff and can be communicated to library users if necessary.

Depending on the organizational and technical structure of the information service, staff not directly engaged in virtual reference transactions with patrons may still be involved in supporting the service. Question routing, customizing forms, transcript and knowledge base management, and other activities are all vital to the successful operation of the service and are examples of tasks that may be performed by reference staff not directly involved in answering questions. As a result, reference staff may be divided into different job groups, which in turn may result in slightly different training programs once the Beginning level has been achieved. Depending on the structure and needs of a particular library or organization, the Intermediate and Advanced levels of training for all reference staff may not be the same. Staff involved in answering patron questions and providing research services, for example, may follow a different training program than their colleagues who do not provide virtual reference assistance. Potential advantages of divergent training programs may include quicker mastery of targeted skills and shorter training sessions, as the content in each program is geared towards building on skills already achieved within the context of a particular job or set of duties. Yet while there may be advantages to such targeted training, administrators should be aware of potential pitfalls as well. Creating divergent, customized training programs for staff within one department can be both time-consuming and complicated. Moreover, staff who receive the same training content and achieve the same levels of competency offer greater flexibility and can provide greater depth of service than departments composed of reference staff at varying skill levels. The individual needs of a reference department dictate its organizational structure and staffing models, and administrators are advised to examine all their training options to see which ones are best suited for their particular institution.

As noted previously, it is recommended that all LIS students in an ALA-accredited Master's program have some exposure to virtual reference. Students should achieve at least the Beginning level competencies through a core reference program and gain the Intermediate or preferably Advanced level through an advanced reference course.

Stages in Creating a Training Program

This section offers guidelines for creating a successful training program for both work and academic environments. The stages and steps outlined here are based on the training phases presented in *The AskA Starter Kit: How to Build and Maintain Digital Reference Services* by David Lankes and Abby Kasowitz (1998), and the Instructional System Design method of training and education as presented by human resource expert Donald Clark (2006).

An effective virtual reference training program involves a great deal of planning and preparation prior to the start of actual training. Successful training programs present a variety of materials, resources, and hands-on activities in order to create a proactive and supportive environment for effective learning to occur. In such an environment, students and staff may be encouraged to explore and think critically about the skills and resources needed for effective virtual reference.

There are three basic stages in creating an effective virtual reference training program for staff and students alike:

- Stage 1: Develop the Training Program.
- Stage 2: Produce the Training Program.
- Stage 3: Implement and Manage the Training Program.

Each of these three stages is further divided into specific components and exercises that are conducted within each stage. In each of the following stages, a brief outline of each stage is presented, along with a fuller description of the steps and activities to be found within that stage.

Stage 1: Develop the Training Program

- establish training goals
- plan and select training elements
- plan for learner assessment

Creating a training program or educational unit requires a great deal of prior planning. Stage 1 focuses on those activities necessary to plan and develop a virtual reference training or education program. There are three steps in this stage.

Establish Training Goals

This step focuses on the following questions:

- What are the instructional goals and objectives of this training program or class unit?
- What are the desired learning outcomes?

Creating a training or education program for its own sake accomplishes little. In creating a virtual reference training program or educational unit, instructors need to decide what information and skills their learners need to acquire in order to effectively perform job duties or meet certain criteria. For reference practitioners, goals may include increased computer literacy, more effective searching techniques, or faster response time to virtual patrons. For LIS faculty, goals for their students may include increased exposure to issues regarding remote reference provision, hands-on experience with virtual reference software, or time spent responding to real patrons in a virtual environment. Whatever an instructor's specific aims might be, establishing training goals is a vital component in developing a training program or unit. The creation of training goals should occur at the beginning of the planning process in developing a training program, because it is the foundation on which the rest of the program will be built.

One of the first steps in determining training goals is to examine the tasks that learners will be expected to perform. The AskA Starter Kit identifies four primary areas of task definition that should be considered when developing a training program:

1. What are the tasks that reference staff members will need to perform their job duties?
2. What skills are required of reference staff members in order to perform these tasks?
3. To what extent are reference staff members prepared to perform these tasks?
4. What will the training program attempt to accomplish in terms of preparing reference staff members to perform these tasks?

1. What are the tasks that reference staff members will need to perform their job duties?

The tasks to be performed by reference staff can be identified through task analysis. Task analysis is important because it examines the fundamental methods by which a specific task or job is performed. It also provides an examination of the frequency, importance, and difficulty of components within tasks (Clark, 2006). Such analysis is important in the development of training or education programs because it helps determine the instructional goals and objectives; e.g., given a particular set of tasks, what is it that learners ought to know in order to perform these tasks? In terms of virtual reference education, this step may be characterized by analyzing the reference department, the virtual reference service, or the virtual reference curriculum of a reference class in order to achieve an understanding of how the department/service works. The resulting analysis can then be used to address a variety of training issues.

While many tasks are outlined in staff job descriptions, the rapidly changing nature of technology and services causes many official descriptions to lag behind actual duties performed by staff. Performing a task analysis on a regular basis is a valuable way to keep job descriptions current, as well as to quickly identify any imminent training needs.

Task analysis also breaks down deceptively simple tasks into individual components that are sometimes quite complex in themselves. For example, responding to a patron inquiry via chat requires several steps, including:

- greeting the patron entering chat queue
- reading the initial patron question
- conducting a reference interview/clarifying information needed
- initiating a search for information on Internet or library databases
- pushing Web pages or escorting patron to sources of information
- asking the patron if information needs are met
- closing the session

These steps show a simple breakdown of a chat session; in reality, sessions may be much more complex, with many more steps taken and more give-and-take between the librarian and patron. Each of the above steps has prompted much research in information science literature. Much has been written, for example, on the difficulties of conducting reference interviews in a digital environment. Many reference staff members also juggle multiple virtual patrons simultaneously, which increases stress and adds to the complexity of the task being performed. One of the benefits of task analysis, then, is to examine all the smaller tasks within a larger task to determine where additional training or education is needed.

Figure 9-2 shows a sample task analysis flow chart that has been adapted from The AskA Starter Kit (p. 83).

Task analysis is beneficial for LIS instructors to perform as well. While many reference courses will not be able to devote as much time to virtual reference as an advanced reference course (or a course devoted exclusively to virtual reference), faculty can use task analysis to help identify a few salient topics within virtual reference on which to focus in class. In addition to an overview of virtual reference services, for example, an instructor may choose to focus on the components of conducting reference interviews with remote users and build hands-on exercises around this particular aspect of virtual reference for the class.

2. What skills are required of reference staff members in order to perform these tasks?

Specific skills for certain tasks may be identified after a task analysis has been completed. Many tasks are likely to be a mixture of higher- and lower-level skills. Conducting an Internet search, for example, involves opening a Web browser (Beginning level skill), selecting an appropriate search engine (Intermediate level skill), and evaluating the accuracy and appropriateness of information presented on a selected Internet site (Advanced level skill). Still other tasks may be readily identified as requiring either basic (beginning), intermediate, or advanced-level skills to be adequately performed by staff or students.

Establishing core competencies for virtual reference prompts the review of learners' existing skills and helps identify gaps between actual proficiency and targeted proficiency levels. Along with the results of a task analysis, instructors can then use this information to plan their training and education programs by identifying the missing skills and knowledge needed for effective and efficient virtual reference.

Figure 9-2: Task Analysis Diagram of a Typical Virtual Reference Transaction

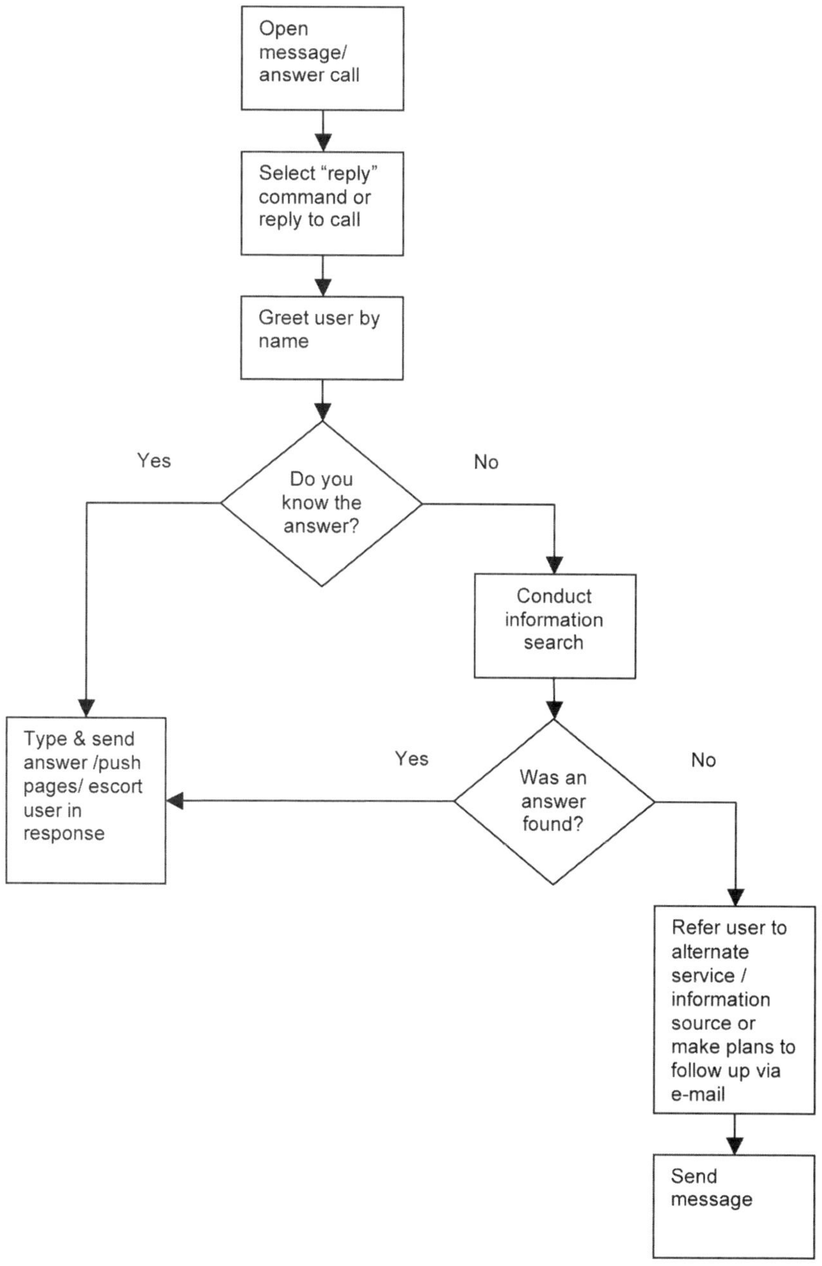

3. To what extent are reference staff members prepared to perform these tasks?

Possessing knowledge of virtual reference issues and methods does not necessarily translate into knowing how to perform virtual reference duties. LIS students who are exposed to virtual reference simply through articles and readings, for example, face just such a dilemma. Even if well-read in current topics and technologies regarding virtual reference service, such students are not yet equipped to provide virtual reference service to patrons. In planning a training and education program, it is essential that instructors determine how well their learners are currently prepared to perform the necessary tasks. Such information can be gathered through surveys, interviews, and other methods. Instructors can use the information garnered to help them identify the level of skills and knowledge that their students and learners currently possess. A few examples of preliminary information to gather from learners might include:

- Familiarity with the user population of the virtual reference service. Do they know who the user population is?
- What specific software applications do the learners know how to use?
- What is their level of comfort and familiarity with the Internet?
- What is their level of comfort and familiarity in conducting online searches?
- Are they able to identify and locate appropriate information resources?
- Do they know basic online etiquette?

Once such preliminary information is gathered and assessed, the instructor can decide whether to institute prerequisite requirements for learners entering the training program or class, or to incorporate any missing skills and/or knowledge into the training program itself.

4. What will the training program attempt to accomplish in terms of preparing reference staff members to perform these tasks?

Once the gap between what learners know and what they need to know is identified, instructors can focus on developing the content of the training program. The goals for each training program can be stated on training materials, and from these goals specific learning objectives can be created. Learning objectives are concrete statements of what training participants will be able to understand and perform at the conclusion of the training program. Goals and learning objectives obviously will differ according to the level of competency targeted by a particular program and the existing skill and knowledge level of the audience. For example, a training program aimed at bringing learners to the Intermediate level of computer literacy in virtual reference may feature goals and objectives such as those listed in Figure 9-3.

Since each level of virtual reference competency outlined in this book builds upon a lower-level competency, prerequisite skills and knowledge may be specified at the outset of the training program. Prerequisite skills may be determined by questionnaires or surveys or may be defined as skills learned in a training program to achieve a previous level of competency.

Figure 9-3: Training Program for an Intermediate Level of Virtual Reference Computer Literacy

Goal:	To develop computer skills consistent with the Intermediate level for digital reference provision

Prerequisites:	Before participating in this training, you should be able to:
	1. Log in to
	   a. Virtual reference software package/IM application
	   b. Library databases
	   c. ftp software
	   d. reference department e-mail
	2. Perform basic searches using library databases and Internet search engines
	3. Download and save files
	4. Upload files
	5. Perform basic commands and key shortcuts in Windows or Mac and VR software
	6. Set and change security levels of Internet cookies as appropriate

Objectives:	At the completion of this training, you will be able to: 1. Understand the differences between various search engines and their respective strengths and weaknesses 2. Formulate effective search strategies 3. Perform additional commands and key shortcuts in Windows or Mac and VR software 4. Perform co-browsing functions with patron 5. Understand some of the features of different types of VR applications and other chat technologies 6. Recognize symptoms of computer viruses and spyware and take measures to eliminate them

Plan and Select Training Elements

Following the establishment of goals in the training program, the second step is to consider what kinds of elements are to be involved in the training. This step focuses on brainstorming, planning, and selection of training materials and activities. At this point, instructors should know their learners' current capabilities and should have identified the gaps in their skills and knowledge that training will address. In order to create and prepare effective training materials, the following components should be reviewed prior to creating training content.

1. Select the tasks to be learned

The training needs for practicing reference staff are largely dictated by the goals and requirements of their department or organization. In order to perform virtual reference tasks efficiently and effectively, staff must demonstrate skills at a certain level. For LIS students, instructors should decide which aspects of virtual reference to focus on. This is especially important if the time allotted to virtual reference topics is short. Tasks identified at the Beginning level of competency will obviously differ from those identified as requiring either Intermediate or Advanced level skills.

2. Choose instructional setting/method for tasks to be learned

The decision where and how the training will take place is important. Training may occur in a variety of settings, such as a classroom, conference room, computer lab, or at home via remote training. Sessions conducted at libraries in areas where virtual reference is provided is an ideal location for training to occur. Here learners can view the actual process of answering questions remotely and at a later date receive hands-on experience in helping virtual patrons.

Instructors also need to decide how the training will be administered. Will training be conducted on-site or at a distance? Will training participants log into a course management system, such as WebCT or Blackboard, or be directed to Web-based manuals and tutorials? Increasing numbers of libraries belong to reference cooperatives, where staff are geographically dispersed and in-person training is not feasible. Distance-education students face similar circumstances and also are likely to participate in training remotely. A hybrid training approach, with both in-person and remote modules, is another possibility for instructors to consider. Some distance education programs, for example, require a brief residency period for face-to-face instruction. See Figure 9-4 for an overview of possible instructional delivery methods.

3. Develop learning objectives for each task

Learning objectives are a critical factor in the design and development of any training program. They help focus the instructor and participants on the skill that is to be learned for a specific task and pave the way for effective assessment. Learning objectives must be consistent with the goals of the training program, clear in their intent, and measurable. Some examples of good learning objectives are:

- By the end of today's session, you will be able to list 3 resources where you can find the gross domestic product of Panama.
- By the end of Tuesday's class, you will be able to successfully demonstrate the co-browse function in our virtual reference software package.
- By the end of today's session, you will be able to successfully log in to the virtual reference system; review the queue of available questions; and claim a question to respond to.

The sequence in which learning objectives are presented is also an important factor to consider when developing a training program or educational unit. Learning objectives that are presented from simplest to most complex allow learners to build on prior knowledge and successes. Other learning objectives may be presented in the order that a job or task demands. For example,

Figure 9-4: Sample Instructional Delivery Methods

Training Method	Discussion	Practice	Feedback	Job Aids*	Comments
Print-based materials		✓		✓	• Good for face-to-face sessions • Does not allow practice in authentic setting but can help to sharpen some skills • Copy and mail costs may be expensive for remote training • Portable—learners can take with them to a variety of settings
Instructor-led presentation (in-person)	✓			✓	• Good for introducing topics; must follow up with review, practice, and feedback • Can be done at conferences, service site, etc.
Instructor-led class (in-person)	✓	✓	✓	✓	• Works if learner and instructor are at same geographic location (i.e., university campus library) • Can cover broader issues of VR • Practice is authentic only if learners have access to necessary technology
One-on-one mentoring	✓	✓	✓	✓	• Allows individual attention to participant's needs and skills • Works in face-to-face or remote situations along with print materials, digital materials, or both

(Cont'd.)

Figure 9-4: Sample Instructional Delivery Methods *(Continued)*					
Training Method	Discussion	Practice	Feedback	Job Aids*	Comments
Web-based instruction	✓ includes Wikis or blogs	✓	✓	✓	• Allows easy access to supplemental information via links • Authentic practice possible through VR packages • Allows access to online resources (i.e., Q&A archives, transcripts)
Course management systems (i.e., Blackboard, WebCT, etc.)	✓	✓	✓	✓	• Can build in assessment models • Allows access to supplemental information and resources

Note: Job Aids are resources that help learners perform tasks by providing access to information, policies, examples, and procedures. Examples of job aids include handouts, checklists, charts, etc. [This table was adapted from "The Possible Treatments and Delivery Tools Matrix" appearing in *The AskA Starter Kit* (1998), pp. 99–100.]

information presented on closing a virtual reference session is bound to be confusing to learners if they have not yet learned how to conduct a virtual reference interview. Presenting learning objectives in the sequence in which the actual task is performed is a much more effective way to structure objectives.

4. Identify and list the steps required to perform the tasks to be learned

The various components of specific virtual reference tasks have likely already been identified through the task analysis. The analysis pinpoints the relevant skills and knowledge needed to successfully accomplish these tasks. By reviewing the task analysis, instructors can develop instructional materials and activities that specifically address the skills necessary to perform these tasks.

5. Develop relevant activities to help participants learn the task

Successful training programs offer effective instructional activities and strategies to further student learning. For example, initiating a partnership with their university libraries may present LIS instructors with opportunities to provide hands-on virtual reference training for their students. The evaluation of actual virtual reference transcripts allows learners to critique how transactions are managed, while Internet "treasure hunts" prompt learners to locate appropriate resources in order to find the requested information. Hands-on activities such as these are vital learning tools and offer information and skills that are not possible to acquire through readings or lectures alone.

Plan for Learner Assessment

Learner assessment is the process of collecting and analyzing feedback provided by training participants in order to gauge how well the learning objectives have been met. Assessment is important because it (1) highlights strengths and weaknesses in the training program and (2) reveals which learners are ready to advance to the next stage of training or competency and which learners need additional training. Many reference departments do not allow staff to perform actual virtual reference transactions until they have achieved a specific level of competency. Still other services assign seasoned staff to monitor responses until all participating staff achieve the desired level of proficiency. While monitoring responses helps ensure a consistent level of service, it is time-consuming and often places an additional burden on staff who are needed to perform other duties.

There are many types of learning assessments, but three that are appropriate for virtual reference training programs are materials-based assessment, performance assessment, and competency-based assessment:

- *Materials-based assessment* is widely used in all areas of education and training and refers to the practice of administering tests to assess competency following the completion of a unit of instruction. This type of assessment can be effective for demonstrating a learner's grasp of certain types of intellectual content but is ineffective for testing the proficiency of skills. Materials-based assessments are simple to administer but do not provide the opportunity to evaluate the actual training process and materials themselves (Lytle and Wolfe, 1989).
- *Performance assessment* involves the direct observation of learners performing a specific task or set of tasks. Such assessments usually are evaluated against performance criteria that have been previously explained and noted in the training program or class. Performance assessment is a good way for learners to demonstrate their abilities by applying their knowledge and skills to a particular task or activity. This type of assessment is effective for the demonstration of hands-on skills by learners, such as conducting a virtual reference interview, performing an online search, and other tasks. Since learners usually are assessed on both the process and the result of their work, instructors can readily identify where in the process a learner needs additional training or support.
- *Competency-based assessment* measures a learner's performance against a clearly defined standard of satisfactory performance. Such assessments are based on a learner's actual performance against specified standards rather than comparing their performance to other learners in the training program or class.

All of the above types of learner assessments have their respective strengths and weaknesses, and an effective training program will not use one type of assessment exclusively. Depending on the skills, tasks, and knowledge to be measured, a blend of learner assessment types is most beneficial to both training participants and instructors alike. It is also important that instructors communicate to learners precisely which types of assessment to expect at various stages in the training.

Stage 2: Produce the Training Program

- develop and sequence learning objectives
- create instructional materials
- develop activities and exercises
- prepare learner assessments and other evaluation measures
- finalize instructional setting and methods

Once the various elements of the training program have been selected, instructional materials and activities can then be created and organized. At this stage in planning, instructors have selected the tasks to be learned, analyzed them, developed goals and learning objectives for the training program participants, selected the instructional setting and delivery method for the program content, and developed an assessment plan for program participants.

Stage 2 in creating a virtual reference training program focuses on the creation and production of instructional materials and activities to be used in the program. There are five steps in this stage.

Develop and Sequence Learning Objectives

Learning objectives serve as the foundation of the training program. They express training goals, communicate the training program's desired outcomes to learners, and provide the basis for evaluation. As mentioned previously, learning objectives must be clearly stated and readily measurable. Each separate section, module, or activity within the training program should state its own particular set of learning objectives.

Instructors must determine the best order in which to present training concepts to their participants or students. In order for learners to build on their acquired knowledge and skills, it is important to structure learning objectives from the simplest to the most complex. Structuring the objectives in this way prompts the instructor to think critically about the types of knowledge, skills, and strategies that learners will need to possess in order to master the objectives.

Create Instructional Materials

Depending on the learning objectives of the training program or unit, some materials may be adapted from existing materials. For a hands-on component of a virtual reference unit, for example, a LIS instructor may be able to use portions of virtual reference training materials used by his/her university library.

Likewise, portions of training materials may, in turn, be used in actual reference provision at a later date. For example, instructions on how to perform various functions within a virtual reference software package may be provided as step-by-step "cheat sheets" for staff members performing virtual reference duties after training occurs.

Effective instructional materials are clearly written and present information in a logical fashion. When preparing instructional materials for virtual reference education, there are a few suggestions to consider:

- *Learning objectives:* It is a good idea to state the learning objectives for each session, class, or unit on any accompanying instructional materials. Students or training participants who can readily view learning objectives on class materials such as worksheets, handouts, and other resources understand what content to expect, as well as what skills or knowledge they are expected to acquire by the end of the session.
- *Present information and concepts clearly:* Like any field of study or employment, virtual reference creates and uses its own specific set of jargon and concepts. LIS instructors should be particularly mindful that students have varying levels of expertise and experience, and that their class may be a student's introduction to virtual reference. Information should be presented in a clear, straightforward fashion, with plenty of examples to help illustrate concepts. The use of real-world examples acquaints learners with the kinds of situations they are likely to encounter and reinforces concepts introduced through readings, lectures, and discussions.

Develop Activities and Exercises

The inclusion of relevant activities and exercises in a training or education program is critical to the success of the program, as it allows learners to apply their conceptual knowledge to perform a task. Authentic activities that attempt to simulate virtual reference experiences allow learners to demonstrate their knowledge and apply problem-solving techniques. Some suggested types of activities include:

- Internet "treasure hunts." Learners are asked to find answers to various types of questions using online resources.
- Reference interview simulations. With one learner posing as a patron and another posing as a librarian, a reference interview can be conducted via e-mail, chat, instant messaging, or through virtual reference software.
- Simulated virtual reference transactions. With one learner posing as a patron, and another acting as a librarian, an entire reference transaction can be conducted via e-mail, chat, instant messaging, or through virtual reference software. At Intermediate and Advanced levels of training, learners posing as librarians can practice responding to two or more simultaneous patrons in real time.

• Transcript analysis. Learners look at transcripts of exemplary, mediocre, and ineffective virtual reference transactions to assess strengths, weaknesses, and what improvements could be made to provide more effective service.

Prepare Learner Assessments and Other Evaluation Measures

One of the steps in Stage 1, Developing the Training Program, describes the process for planning for learner assessments. In that stage, instructors consider which type of assessment (materials-based, performance-based, competency-based, etc.) or blend of assessments may be best used for their training and education programs. At this point, instructors can create their assessments based on the types of knowledge and skills that they want their students and participants to acquire. Materials-based assessments, for example, are perhaps best used for testing theoretical concepts and factual information, while either performance- or competency-based evaluation is most effective for the demonstration of specific skills and knowledge, such as conducting an effective reference interview or pushing Web pages to a virtual patron.

While the primary function of learner assessments is to evaluate how well students and participants have absorbed the information presented in the training, the assessments also can be used to evaluate the effectiveness of the training program itself. If a significant number of learners demonstrate difficulty using the co-browse feature during a performance-based assessment, for example, then the instructor can note that more time needs to be devoted to this feature in the training program. Learner assessments, then, can provide the instructor with the opportunity to gauge which parts of the training program are effective and which parts may need to be revised.

It is also possible to incorporate an area within an assessment to solicit learner feedback about the training. Such feedback provides the instructor with information not necessarily about which content the learners enjoyed the most, but the methods and activities that helped them learn the material most effectively. Good virtual reference training is always fluid, and uses both evaluation and feedback to make changes when necessary to meet learner needs. Additional information on soliciting learner feedback is discussed in a later section.

Finalize Instructional Setting and Methods

In Stage 1, Developing the Training Program, instructors are asked to consider where they will hold their training and education sessions and by which method(s) they will deliver the training. At this point in the training program preparations, the instructional setting—or settings—and methods of instructional delivery should be finalized.

At this stage in the planning, any outstanding issues should be resolved. For example, if the training is part of a distance education course, will course management systems be involved? Has an agreement been reached with the university library to provide some hands-on demonstrations and experience for learners? Are there any question-answering entities that offer volunteer opportunities in which reference students or staff can hone their skills? The Internet Public Library, for example, offers training and volunteer opportunities for University of Michigan LIS students. Is there a similar organization willing to offer virtual reference experience for your students?

Most instructors use a mixture of instructional methods and delivery tools. Traditional print-based materials such as training guides, articles, and the like are often offered alongside Web-based instruction through online discussion groups, blogs, and other means. There are inherent strengths and challenges presented by all types of instructional delivery methods, and Figure 9-5 highlights some factors to consider when preparing different types of training methods:

Figure 9-5: Potential Issues in Various Instructional Methods

Training Method	Technical Issues	Skills	Aesthetic & Performance Issues
Print-based materials	Photocopies; printing & binding of materials; mailing and distribution; copyright concerns	Writing and formatting	Balance of text and graphics; photocopy quality
Instructor-led presentation or class (in-person)	Confirm availability of equipment (e.g., LCD or overhead projector); Internet connection; seating, etc.	Presentation and teaching skills; ability to use presentation software; operation of equipment	Presentation software offers many various graphic design opportunities; ability to link to the Web; audio component available
E-mail	Collecting participants' e-mail addresses; ISP attachment/filter concerns	Possible use of listservs or other discussion list software	Use of "vanilla" formatting to accommodate display in various e-mail packages
One-on-one mentoring (in-person)	Can both people share a computer, or does each need their own? Physical space for both people	Interpersonal skills; ability to adapt training delivery to different learners' needs	
Web-based instruction	Secure Web space; issues with pop-up blockers; participant connection speeds	Knowledge of HTML or Web editing software; Wiki or blog management skills	Balance of text and graphics

(Cont'd)

Figure 9-5: Potential Issues in Various Instructional Methods
(Continued)

Training Method	Technical Issues	Skills	Aesthetic & Performance Issues
Course management systems (i.e., Blackboard, WebCT, etc.)	Collecting participants' e-mail addresses and information	Knowledge of course management software and tools	Ability to customize colors, graphics, display of text, location of files, etc.

This figure was adapted from "Issues in Preparing Delivery Tools" appearing in *The AskA Starter Kit* by Lankes and Kasowitz (1998), p. 110.

Stage 3: Implement and Manage the Training Program

- Schedule and conduct training sessions and activities
- Provide feedback to learners
- Evaluate and revise the training program

Up to this point, Stages 1 and 2 have focused on selecting and organizing the training content, preparing materials, settling on an instructional setting, and other factors. Stage 3 focuses on the actual implementation and management of the virtual reference training and education program. There are three steps in this stage.

Schedule and Conduct Training Sessions and Activities

Scheduling training sessions for reference staff can be fraught with problems. Conflicts in staff schedules are inevitable and can be difficult to work around. The reference desk must remain staffed, virtual and telephone reference services must be performed, and so forth. As a result, some training sessions may need to be offered more than once so that all pertinent staff may attend. Still other scheduling conflicts can be avoided by offering competency-based training. Staff training to achieve the Intermediate level of competency in computer literacy, for example, leaves staff at both the Beginning and Advanced levels remaining to keep reference operations running during the training session.

For on-site LIS instructors and students, scheduling may present fewer challenges. Reference classes meet at assigned times and days, and training sessions may be conducted during class. For distance-education students, LIS instructors may need to practice some degree of flexibility in drawing up training sessions. Many distance education students have full-time jobs and family commitments to work around, and their availability may be limited. In such cases, the instructor can post a list of dates and times for training sessions and have students select which ones best fit their schedules. It is best to offer a variety of days and times (some evening sessions, for example) so that everyone is able to participate. Remembering that distance education students may be in different time zones also is important.

While hands-on exercises are often best conducted during the actual training session, some exercises may be completed as homework. Searching exercises, such as Internet treasure hunts and database searches, are examples of good homework assignments. Learners also may answer a series of increasingly difficult practice questions for homework in order to practice their skills before attempting to respond to real patrons.

Provide Feedback to Learners

Good training programs provide learners with enough useful information, guidance, and peer support to motivate them to continue to practice and apply the skills and knowledge learned after the training program has been completed. Providing feedback to learners and training participants is a vital component in any training program. Constructive feedback is almost always appreciated by students and other learners. In addition to providing positive support for the improvement of their skills and abilities, constructive feedback also provides personal attention by acknowledging each learner's trials and accomplishments in learning the training material.

There are several elements to consider when providing constructive feedback:

- *Emphasize the positive*—constructive feedback affirms each learner's progress and achievements and does not dwell on weaknesses. Everyone makes mistakes, and all learners master new skills at varying rates. Acknowledging obstacles that have been overcome rather than how long it may have taken to overcome them encourages learners to persevere in their training and to take ownership of their learning.

- *Timeliness*—constructive feedback should be given to learners in time to help them in their next task

- *Make specific and detailed statements*—clear communication is vital when giving feedback. Ambiguous feedback is sometimes given by instructors who are either unaccustomed to or uncomfortable with providing feedback. Ambiguous feedback benefits neither student nor instructor and can derail any training or education program. Clear and detailed feedback, then, is essential if learners are to understand what their strengths and weaknesses are and how they can improve their performance. An example of feedback that clearly discusses a specific concern might read something like this:

  > This was a great first effort! You remembered to address the patron by name, gave him cues as to when you were searching and approximately how long it would take to find the information, and found some good information for him. One thing you forgot was to cite your sources—this is an important step to remember in the future, as your patron will likely need to include this information in his research.

• *Provide tips or suggestions on how to improve performance*—feedback is most useful when it suggests how to improve performance or utility. For example:

> One suggestion to improve the readability of your response regarding Costa Rica's climate is to increase your use of white space, like this:
> "You can find information about Costa Rica's climate at the Costa Rica Information page at:
>
> http://centralamerica.com/cr/info/
>
> This resource says that Costa Rica is "a tropical country which contains several distinct climatic zones. There is no winter or summer as such and most regions have a rainy season from May to November and a dry season from December to April. Annual rainfall averages 100 inches nationwide with some mountainous regions getting as much as 25 feet on exposed eastern slopes. Temperature is more a matter of elevation than location with a mean of around 72 degrees in the Central Valley, 82 degrees on the Atlantic coast and 89 degrees on the Pacific coast."

• *Feedback is a learning tool as well as an evaluative too*—while many instructors view feedback as one of the final components in a training or education program, it is more effective to use feedback from the outset of the training. When used consistently throughout a training program, constructive feedback can become an effective catalyst for active learning by prompting students to question and explore the material more fully. The use of feedback simply to note whether students were correct or incorrect in some process or knowledge does little or nothing to engage them in the learning process.

Feedback can be given either orally or in writing and does not necessarily have to be a formal endeavor. Simply asking learners if they have any questions on material just covered helps solicit feedback, as well as aids in creating a supportive learning environment.

Evaluate and Revise the Training Program

Most instructors understand the value of ongoing evaluation to their training and education programs. Virtual reference is a swiftly changing field, with new types of capabilities and technical advancements appearing each year. Training and education programs need to adapt their focus and materials on an ongoing basis in order to provide the most effective training possible.

Evaluation efforts can range from the informal (e.g., verbal discussion with learners, simple observation) to the formal, such as written surveys or questionnaires. There also are a host of convenient online survey instruments, such as those found at Zoomerang.com, QuestionPro.com, SurveyMonkey.com, and others. To create effective assessments, instructors need to focus on exactly what kinds of information they want to solicit from their learners. Some items to consider when creating an assessment tool may include:

Why is the training being evaluated?
- Feedback for course improvement
- Determination of training program effectiveness
- Demonstration of learner competency
- Demonstration of learner progression

What will be evaluated?
- Training materials
- Training content
- Facilities/equipment
- Instructor
- Achievement of target skills/knowledge
- Time allotted for unit/training program

What types of measurement will be used?
- Measurement scales (Strongly Agree, Often, No Opinion, Disagree, Strongly Disagree; Excellent, Good, Fair, Poor, etc.)
- Open-ended questions
- Multiple-choice questions
- Essay

Once the assessments have been completed or noted, the results should be reviewed and analyzed. Based on the information provided by the evaluations, the content, supporting materials, exercises, and other components of the training program or educational unit can then be revised as necessary. Although many evaluation tools tend to be generic so they can be applied in different contexts, instructors can adapt existing evaluations to solicit learner feedback on specific aspects of training. The following sample evaluation tool (see Figure 9-6) can be adapted for either a training program or reference course.

Figure 9-6: Sample Evaluation Tool for a Virtual Reference Training Program or LIS Course

INSTRUCTIONS

Your feedback is important to us. It helps us evaluate the effectiveness of this training program and make changes as necessary. Thank you!

Training Program Title: _____

Instructor: _____

Participant Name (optional): _____

Date: _____

(Cont'd.)

Figure 9-6: Sample Evaluation Tool for a Virtual Reference Training Program or LIS Course *(Continued)*

Scale ratings:

N/A=Not Applicable, 1=Strongly Disagree, 2=Disagree, 3=Not sure, 4=Agree, 5=Strongly Agree

Please circle your response for each item:

PROGRAM CONTENT

I was aware of the prerequisites for this program	N/A 1 2 3 4 5
I had the prerequisite skills/knowledge for this program	N/A 1 2 3 4 5
I understood the program's objectives	N/A 1 2 3 4 5
The content was relevant to my job	N/A 1 2 3 4 5
The program's activities gave me sufficient practice	N/A 1 2 3 4 5
The program's materials (handouts, etc.) were helpful	N/A 1 2 3 4 5
The program's activities stimulated my learning	N/A 1 2 3 4 5

PROGRAM DESIGN

The program's goals and objectives were clearly stated	N/A 1 2 3 4 5
The program's pace was appropriate	N/A 1 2 3 4 5
The content was presented in a logical order	N/A 1 2 3 4 5

PROGRAM RESULTS

I accomplished the objectives of this program	N/A 1 2 3 4 5
This program was worth my time	N/A 1 2 3 4 5
I will be able to use what I learned in this program	N/A 1 2 3 4 5
I feel confident in using my new skills	N/A 1 2 3 4 5

PROGRAM INSTRUCTOR

The instructor was well-prepared	N/A 1 2 3 4 5
The instructor was knowledgeable about the material	N/A 1 2 3 4 5
The instructor motivated me to do my best work	N/A 1 2 3 4 5
The instructor solicited feedback from participants	N/A 1 2 3 4 5
The instructor satisfactorily responded to feedback	N/A 1 2 3 4 5

(Cont'd.)

Figure 9-6: Sample Evaluation Tool for a Virtual Reference Training Program or LIS Course *(Continued)*

What other improvements could you suggest for this program?

_____
_____
_____
_____
_____

What was most valuable about this training program?

_____
_____
_____
_____
_____

What was least valuable about this training program?

_____
_____
_____
_____
_____

Core Competencies for Virtual Reference

This section discusses the need for LIS instructors and reference departments to integrate core competencies for virtual reference into their existing curricula and training programs. The DREI Board outlined 10 areas of competency to be taught at three different levels: Beginning (with a focus on skills to be attained); Intermediate (focusing on the conceptual understanding of skills to be performed); and Advanced (developing an administrative focus of tasks to be performed). The 10 areas of competency discussed in this section are:

- Computer Literacy
- Virtual Reference Software
- Virtual Reference Encountering or Interview
- Digital Information Resources Creation and Use
- Evaluation of Services
- Policies and Procedures
- Instructional Role
- Triage and Collaboration
- Virtual Reference Community
- Knowledge Base Acquisition and Use

These competencies have been developed both to guide virtual reference instruction in MLIS programs and aid in the training, hiring, and evaluation of practicing librarians and staff with virtual reference responsibilities.

Computer Literacy

Computer literacy has become increasingly important over the past decade for the general population, but especially for librarians and other information providers. While most librarians in public service positions routinely answer all types of hardware and software questions, reference librarians are now often required to respond to all manner of computer issues, as well as perform digital reference duties. This technological shift has created a demand for competent staff that can adapt quickly and positively to technological change. The ever-increasing technological demands also have highlighted a need for computer literacy standards for reference positions. By its very nature, virtual reference demands technical competence. The term "computer literacy" has various definitions and applications, but for the purposes of this workbook, computer literacy may be defined as the knowledge and ability to use computers effectively in performing tasks.

In the DREI rubrics for digital reference providers, the computer literacy competency focuses on a practitioner's ability to:

- Perform basic computer actions in order to facilitate digital reference encounters
- Adapt to different software requirements and platforms
- Formulate criteria and evaluate performance

Establishing core competencies for computer literacy allows librarians and administrators determine what necessary skills are lacking and where additional training is needed.

Competency in Computer Literacy: Beginning Level

At the Beginning level for competency in computer literacy, the requirements focus on attaining proficiency in the basic skills needed for providing virtual reference. Although these skills may vary by institution, in general such skills include:

- Login
- Computer commands
- Search operators
- Uploading data
- Protocols
- Navigating proxy servers
- Downloading data
- Keyboarding skills
- Basic troubleshooting skills

All manner of virtual reference software packages, databases, and some Web sites require users to log in and perform various commands to access resources or navigate through the software. Adequate keyboarding skills also are essential, particularly for staff engaged in chat reference or other types of virtual reference. Patrons using chat reference and instant messaging expect near-instantaneous responses from librarians, and the pressure on reference staff to provide good service quickly can be exacerbated by poor typing skills.

Reference staff and LIS students at the Beginning level for competency in computer literacy should be able to perform basic search functions in their local online catalogs, licensed databases, and on the Internet. At this level, staff reliance on a popular search engine such as Google (www.google.com) may be sufficient for their duties, but reference practitioners at higher levels of competency need to be aware of how different search engines can be used most effectively in locating high-quality and relevant information for their patrons.

Protocols allow different types of computer platforms and systems to communicate and exchange information with each other. Although computer protocols have become increasingly invisible to the user, it is still necessary to be able to identify, understand, and to use common protocols such as http, pop, ftp, and others. If responding to patron questions by e-mail, for example, staff may be required to attach articles, photographs, or other information to their responses. Some e-mail packages require users to first upload data to the e-mail server before it can be attached to a message. Other resources may require users to download information from the host computer or database to their local systems to view it on their own workstations.

Proxy servers generally provide two primary functions: As a filter and as a short-term data warehouse. Proxy servers that serve as filters are used by organizations who want to limit access to some or all of their online resources. For example, a university library may require off-campus students to log in through a proxy server to access library resources. Since matriculated students log in with their valid usernames and passwords, unauthorized users are filtered out and cannot access the resources remotely. Other proxy servers act as storage facilities between a host computer and a computer attempting to access information on the host computer. When popular files are continually requested over the Internet, proxy servers can gather and cache these files to lessen the burden on the host computer. The result is much faster access to information for the user. Reference staff at the beginning and higher levels of competency in computer literacy need to know how to help their user communities navigate proxy servers and their attendant issues.

The Beginning Level of the computer literacy competency also requires reference staff to solve common hardware and software problems at a basic level. Some typical troubleshooting capabilities might include:

- knowing how to manage Internet cookies and simple firewall issues
- ability to suggest solutions to virtual patrons who are experiencing difficulties with virtual reference software or remote access to databases
- managing frozen screens and disconnects
- clearing Web browser's cache

Competence in basic troubleshooting skills such as those outlined above and others serves to improve reference staff's ability to resolve technical issues.

Fewer technical glitches result in improved satisfaction for patrons and reference staff alike.

Below is a sample worksheet (Figure 9-7) outlining some computer literacy competencies at the Beginning level. This worksheet can be used as is or adapted for any virtual reference training program or LIS course in which virtual reference is taught. (Note: This worksheet is a general guide only and is meant to be used in conjunction with your own class and/or training content. It should be tailored to your specific needs and technologies.)

Figure 9-7: Sample Computer Literacy Worksheet— Beginning Level	
Goal:	To acquire computer skills and knowledge consistent with the Beginning level for virtual reference
Prerequisites:	Before participating in this training, you should be able to: 1. Open and close software applications 2. Open and save files 3. Connect to the Internet with a Web browser 4. Manage two or more open application windows 5. Access library databases 6. Organize files in directories

Objectives:	At the completion of this training, you will be able to:
	
	1. Log in to:
	   a. virtual reference software package/IM application
	   b. library databases
	   c. ftp software
	   d. reference department e-mail
	   e. course management system (if applicable)
	2. Perform assigned searches using library databases and multiple Internet search engines
	3. Download four sample files from assigned sites and save them to assigned locations on your local system
	4. Upload four sample files from your local system to assigned locations
	5. Connect to sites through a proxy server (if applicable)
	6. Demonstrate discussed basic commands and key shortcuts in Windows or Mac
	7. How to set and change security levels of Internet cookies

Competency in Computer Literacy: Intermediate Level
Once students and practitioners have achieved the Basic level in computer literacy, it is time to move on to achieving the Intermediate level. Whereas the Beginning level of the computer literacy competency focuses on the development of basic technological skills, the Intermediate level emphasizes the development of conceptual skills relating to technology. As previously mentioned, reference practitioners and LIS students at the Intermediate level are assumed to have mastered all skills associated with the Beginning level of the competency. At the Intermediate level, learners are expected to develop an increased understanding of the underlying concepts of technology and display greater flexibility in dealing with systems and software. Thus, in addition to the basics outlined above at the Beginning level, reference staff at the Intermediate level are also expected to demonstrate:

- The ability to perform basic computer actions at the appropriate level required for his or her job
- The ability to adapt to new or different software requirements and platforms

In any training program for virtual reference, a discussion, and preferably demonstration, of different types of question-answering software for e-mail, chat, instant messaging, or other virtual reference software is highly desirable. While many libraries and other information organizations have access to only one type of virtual reference software, software vendors often will feature demonstrations or offer free trials via their company Web sites. While a hands-on demonstration is best, Web-based Flash demonstrations available at some vendor sites still give users an idea of how various software packages function. There are many, many software options to choose from, but some vendors of popular virtual reference software packages currently include:

Altarama RefTracker: www.altarama.com.au/reftrack.htm
Docutek: www.docutek.com/products/vrlplus/trial.html (offers free trial)
OCLC QuestionPoint: www.questionpoint.org/
Tutor.com's Ask a Librarian software: http://tutor.com/products/ aal_technology.aspx

For chat reference:

ConferenceRoom: www.webmaster.com/ (offers free trial)
GoToAssist (formerly Desktopstreaming): www.gotoassist.com (offers free trial)
Liveperson: www.liveperson.com
LiveAssistance: www.liveassistance.com/ (offers free trial)
Trillian: www.ceruleanstudios.com/

Usually, it is possible to arrange for free demonstrations of virtual reference products by vendors who do not offer free trials of their software. Such demonstrations can be particularly helpful for LIS students in comparing features among different systems and seeing what is available in the virtual reference market.

Providing virtual reference also requires a great degree of familiarity with Internet search engines and their respective strengths and weaknesses. While most search engines function very much alike, there are sometimes differences among various engines with which learners should become acquainted. Although Google (www.google.com) currently boasts the largest indexing capability of any Internet search engine, other search engines may produce better and more efficient results, depending on the type of information being sought. Meta-search engines, federated search engines, and engines that cluster results all have their place and sometimes are a better choice than the ubiquitous Google.

It also should be noted that, as technical proficiency increases, learner confidence also grows. Such confidence helps staff and LIS students overcome any resistance or fear of new technologies quicker. The ability to master technical procedures and challenges, and the resulting confidence in their abilities to meet such challenges, helps learners adapt to new technical demands more readily in the future. Throughout their careers, librarians will be confronted with new technologies and different types of software. Regular training and exposure to information on emerging technologies can help them adapt more quickly to new or different software requirements and platforms.

Below is a sample worksheet (Figure 9-8) outlining some computer literacy competencies at the Intermediate level. This worksheet can be used as is or adapted for any virtual reference training program or LIS course in which virtual reference is taught. (Note: This worksheet is a general guide only and is

Figure 9-8: Sample Computer Literacy Worksheet—Intermediate Level	
Goal:	To develop computer skills and knowledge consistent with the Intermediate level for virtual reference

Prerequisites:	Before participating in this training, you should be able to:
	7. Log in to
	  a. virtual reference software package/IM application
	  b. library databases
	  c. ftp software
	  d. reference department e-mail
	  e. course management systems (if applicable)
	8. Perform basic searches using library databases and Internet search engines
	9. Download and save files
	10. Upload files
	11. Perform basic commands and key shortcuts in Windows or Mac and VR software
	12. Set and change security levels of Internet cookies as appropriate

(Cont'd.)

**Figure 9-8: Sample Computer Literacy Worksheet—
Intermediate Level** *(Continued)*

Objectives:	At the completion of this training, you will be able to:
	7. Understand the differences between various search engines and their respective strengths and weaknesses
	8. Formulate effective search strategies
	9. Perform additional commands and key shortcuts in Windows or Mac and VR software
	10. Perform co-browsing functions with patron
	11. Understand some of the features of different types of VR applications and other chat technologies
	12. Recognize symptoms of computer viruses and spyware and take measures to eliminate them

meant to be used in conjunction with your own class and/or training content. It should be tailored to your specific needs and technologies.)

Competency in Computer Literacy: Advanced Level

The concept of administration and applied knowledge is at the center of the Advanced level of competency in computer literacy. At this level, the focus is on developing a deep understanding of technological concepts, as well as the ability to apply critical thinking and problem-solving techniques to using technology.

At the Advanced level, reference staff members and LIS students are expected to demonstrate proficiency in the skills at the Beginning and Intermediate levels, as well as some additional higher-level skills. As a result, at the Advanced level, they should be able to:

- Perform basic computer actions at the appropriate level required for the job
- Adapt to different software requirements and platforms
- Formulate specific competency criteria
- Evaluate performance based on specific criteria

At the Advanced level, reference staff members should be capable of assessing the value of various technologies, as well as the ideas surrounding them. Either as part of a task force or as administrators, library staff members are frequently called upon to evaluate technology and make decisions regarding the cost, need for, and value of implementing certain technologies within their organizations. Establishing computer literacy competencies in an organization helps ensure that the staff is sufficiently educated about and skilled in technology to make effective decisions.

The following sample worksheet (Figure 9-9) outlines some computer literacy competencies at the Advanced level. This worksheet can be used as is or can be adapted for any virtual reference training program or LIS course in which virtual reference is taught. (Note: This worksheet is a general guide only

Figure 9-9: Sample Computer Literacy Worksheet—Advanced Level	
Goal:	To develop computer skills and knowledge consistent with the Advanced level for virtual reference
Prerequisites:	Before participating in this training, you should be able to: 1. Describe the strengths, weaknesses, and differences among seven assigned Internet search engines 2. Formulate effective search strategies 3. Perform co-browsing functions with a patron 4. Understand some of the features of different types of VR applications and other chat technologies 5. Recognize symptoms of computer viruses and spyware and take measures to eliminate them
Objectives:	At the completion of this training, you will be able to: 1. Formulate assessments of the possible benefits and challenges of new technologies to the organization 2. Evaluate staff technical performance 3. Identify staff who require additional training 4. Offer suggestions and solutions for troubleshooting common digital reference and database software problems 5. Revise and develop new computer literacy competencies as needed

and is meant to be used in conjunction with your own class and/or training content. It should be tailored to your specific needs and technologies.)

Virtual Reference Software

Providing virtual reference can require several different types of software. While chat software and other types of real-time technologies have proliferated in recent years, old standbys such as e-mail and Web-based forms are still heavily used in many libraries. As a result, LIS students and reference staff need to be familiar with a variety of methods in which to respond to patron inquiries.

In the DREI rubrics for virtual reference providers, the virtual reference software competency focuses on a practitioner's abilities to:

- demonstrate increasing levels of technical proficiency with local virtual reference software
- comprehend various features of different virtual reference technologies and software
- apply conceptual knowledge of virtual reference software to help evaluate future software and assist in software selection

Competency in Virtual Reference Software: Beginning Level
The requirements for the Beginning level for competency in virtual reference software focus on attaining the basic skills needed to provide virtual reference services. By the end of the training or education program for the Beginning level, learners should be able to:

- demonstrate a basic level of proficiency with their local virtual reference software package
- report any problems with the software in adequate detail to the appropriate contact personnel

While specific skills may vary according to the type of virtual reference software package or technology used, in general such skills include the ability to:

- log in and out of the virtual reference software
- open a new virtual reference interaction
- navigate software features and understand their respective functions
- use canned messages appropriately
- end a virtual reference transaction
- recognize the difference between local and consortial software applications or aspects of such differences in one software application
- transfer questions to another operator or level in the consortial network

One of the goals in establishing competencies for virtual reference is to help all reference staff and LIS students interested in reference work gain a clear understanding of the software used to support their reference service. Virtual reference has become an integral part of most academic, public, and corporate reference departments, and reference providers need to understand how their virtual reference software impacts the specific policies, goals, and guidelines for their services.

The following sample worksheet (Figure 9-10) outlines some virtual reference software competencies at the Beginning level. This worksheet can be used as is or adapted for any virtual reference training program or LIS course in which virtual reference is taught. (Note: This worksheet is a general guide only, and is meant to be used in conjunction with your own class and/or training content. It should be tailored to your specific needs and technologies.)

Competency in Virtual Reference Software: Intermediate Level
Depending on the structure of LIS programs and courses, some students may only gain a Beginning-level competency in virtual reference software. Due to the large number of libraries providing virtual reference services and the competitive job market, it is recommended that LIS students achieve at least the Intermediate level, or preferably Advanced level, of competency in virtual reference software through an elective or advanced reference course.

Figure 9-10: Sample Virtual Reference Software Worksheet—Beginning Level	
Goal:	To develop skills and knowledge regarding virtual reference software that is consistent with the Beginning level for virtual reference
Prerequisites:	Before participating in this training, you should be able to: 1. Open and close software applications 2. Open and save files 3. Connect to the Internet with a Web browser 4. Manage two or more open application windows 5. Access library databases 6. Organize files in directories
Objectives:	At the completion of this training, you will be able to: 1. Log in and out of a selected VR software package 2. Open a virtual reference query 3. Navigate various features in the VR software and have a basic understanding of the function of each featurße 4. Use canned messages appropriately 5. Successfully engage and respond to patron inquiries via VR package (single patron at a time) 6. Transfer questions to another operator or level in the consortial network 7. End a transaction in the software

Learners with an Intermediate-level competency in virtual reference software demonstrate a more detailed understanding of the major concepts pertaining to the software and digital reference than they did at the Beginning level of competency. In addition to the skills and concepts outlined above at the Beginning level, LIS students and reference staff at the Intermediate level of competency in virtual reference software are also expected to demonstrate:

- a higher level of understanding of the features in various virtual reference software packages
- comprehensive knowledge of all operator features of one piece of virtual reference software
- facility with local virtual reference software

By the conclusion of training at the Intermediate level, skills include the ability to:

- recognize which features are similar among various virtual reference packages

- know how local and consortial portions of the software relate to each other
- understand how changes to the software might be desirable and can communicate what those changes should be
- understand how such changes to the software might improve service to users
- utilize more complex software features, such as co-browser and address books
- manage multiple users in a queue
- adapt to changes to the software made within one's institution
- understand any limitations to the virtual reference software and know how to work around them
- provide preliminary triage for virtual reference software problems before reporting to a contact person (at both local and consortial level, if applicable)
- assist other operators one-on-one with users of the virtual reference software
- change modes of communication, if appropriate, for an inquiry, i.e., from chat to e-mail

Below is a sample worksheet (Figure 9-11) outlining some competencies for virtual reference software at the Intermediate level. This worksheet can

Figure 9-11: Sample Virtual Reference Software Worksheet—Intermediate Level	
Goal:	To develop skills and knowledge regarding virtual reference software that is consistent with the Intermediate level for virtual reference
Prerequisites:	Before participating in this training, you should be able to: 1. Log in and out of selected VR software package 2. Open a virtual reference interaction 3. Navigate various features in the VR software and have a basic understanding of the function of each feature 4. Use canned messages appropriately 5. End a transaction in the software 6. Successfully engage and respond to patron inquiries via VR package (single patron at a time) 7. Transfer questions to another operator or level in the consortial network 8. Understand how to report VR software problems in adequate detail to an appropriate contact person 9. Successfully claim and respond to patron inquiries via e-mail

(Cont'd.)

Figure 9-11: Sample Virtual Reference Software Worksheet—Intermediate Level *(Continued)*	
Objectives:	At the completion of this training, you will be able to: 1. Demonstrate the use of co-browser and address book features in VR package 2. Provide preliminary triage and basic troubleshooting for common VR software problems (disconnects, co-browse glitches, etc.) 3. Demonstrate discussed key shortcuts in VR software 4. Manage three simultaneous patrons in queue 5. Switch between VR package and e-mail for patron responses 6. Discuss which features perform similar functions among various VR software packages

be used as is or can be adapted for any virtual reference training program or LIS course in which virtual reference is taught. (Note: This worksheet is a general guide only and is meant to be used in conjunction with your own class and/or training content. It should be tailored to your specific needs and technologies.)

Competency in Virtual Reference Software: Advanced Level

At the Advanced level of the virtual software competency, LIS students and reference staff exhibit a deeper understanding of the major components and applications of the virtual reference software. At this level, learners possess increased facility with the software and think critically about its capabilities and performance. As a result, LIS students and reference staff can articulate their findings and apply them to the evaluation of other software tools, or mentor a colleague in the software's applications. At this level, learners are expected to achieve the following skills and knowledge:

- understand how virtual reference software relates to other issues such as policy, communication, and service
- demonstrate thorough knowledge of virtual reference software in use at one's institution, both locally and consortially, if applicable
- understand the relation between local policy, consortial policy, and the chosen software
- have basic understanding of administrative functions of the software and assist with administration of the software as required
- apply conceptual knowledge of virtual reference software to assist with the evaluation of software selection and to recommend acquisition and implementation

• keep current on trends and developments in virtual reference software products and technologies

Below is a sample worksheet (Figure 9-12) outlining some competencies for virtual reference software at the Advanced level. This worksheet can be used as is or adapted for any virtual reference training program or LIS course in which virtual reference is taught. (Note: This worksheet is a general guide only and is meant to be used in conjunction with your own class and/or training content. It should be tailored to your specific needs and technologies.)

Figure 9-12: Sample Virtual Reference Software Worksheet—Advanced Level	
Goal:	To develop skills and knowledge regarding virtual reference software that is consistent with the Advanced level for virtual reference
Prerequisites:	Before participating in this training, you should be able to: 1. Successfully open and end a transaction in the VRD software 2. Demonstrate proficiency with co-browse and address book features 3. Manage three simultaneous patrons in a queue 4. Use canned messages appropriately 5. Demonstrate common key shortcuts in VR software 6. Easily switch between a VR package and e-mail for patron responses 7. Provide preliminary triage and basic troubleshooting for common VR software problems (disconnects, co-browse glitches, etc.)
Objectives:	At the completion of this training, you will be able to: 1. Produce service statistics via VR software 2. Change passwords and add operators within VR software 3. Install and configure VR software on additional computers 4. Write or edit VR software documentation for colleagues (under supervision) 5. Think critically about the software and its capabilities and articulate opinions to others 6. Train other operators on a VR software package

Virtual Reference Encountering or Interview

Conducting an effective reference interview is perhaps the single most challenging aspect of providing virtual reference service. Reference staff members cannot rely on auditory or visual cues to help assess the user's information needs as they can in face-to-face reference transactions. In fact, virtual librarians' exclusive reliance on the written word can generate all sorts of problems. Remote users who are in a hurry, for instance, may type quickly and make many typographical errors in their inquiries for information. Young adults and children rely heavily on abbreviated forms of writing, which can be all but indecipherable to reference staff unaccustomed to such "netspeak." All of these factors can cause miscommunication and quickly derail a reference interview, frustrating both the librarian and the user.

One unfortunate response by some librarians to virtual service has been simply to disregard the reference interview and instead make assumptions regarding patrons' information needs. One study found that these librarians disliked the increased time it took to type questions and responses to clarify users' requests, and that their discomfort with the electronic medium caused them to end transactions with remote patrons as quickly as possible (Leveen, 2001).

It is no wonder, then, that the advent of virtual reference has shed new light on the importance of the reference interview. Virtual reference experience has suggested adaptations and creative solutions that can be applied to overcome the lack of visual and auditory signals. In the DREI rubrics for virtual reference providers, the virtual reference encounter or interview competency focuses on practitioners' abilities to:

- assess patrons' information-seeking behavior
- compensate for nonverbal cues
- develop effective elicitation techniques
- cultivate online etiquette and politeness
- build good relationships with online patrons
- develop an increased awareness of the formulation of answers and their presentation

Competency in Virtual Reference Encounter or Interview: Beginning Level

The rapid growth of virtual reference services at many institutions attests to their popularity with patrons, and usage statistics for these services continue to climb each year. Patrons like the convenience of not having to be physically present in the library to receive information assistance, and many appreciate the anonymity inherent in a digital environment. Yet, despite these and other advantages, most virtual reference transactions take longer to complete than face-to-face or telephone transactions (Horn, 2001). LIS students and reference staff at the Beginning level of competency in virtual reference encounters or interviews should be reminded that the reference interview needs to be conducted in a slightly different manner than in face-to-face transactions. They should also be reminded that virtual interviewing techniques may take more time than they anticipate, and that effective virtual interviews cannot use shortcuts.

By the end of the training or education program for the Beginning level, learners should be able to:

- follow basic instructions as listed by their reference department
- adapt to unexpected situations
- assist patrons in applying critical thinking skills to searches

Below is a sample worksheet (Figure 9-13) outlining some virtual reference interview competencies at the Beginning level. This worksheet can be used as is or adapted for any virtual reference training program or LIS course in which virtual reference is taught. (Note: This worksheet is a general guide only and is meant to be used in conjunction with your own class and/or training content. It should be tailored to your specific needs and technologies.)

Figure 9-13: Sample Virtual Reference Encounter or Interview Worksheet—Beginning Level	
Goal:	To develop interviewing or encountering skills and knowledge consistent with the Beginning level for virtual reference
Prerequisites:	Before participating in this training, you should be able to: 1. Navigate library databases, VR software, and/or course management system (if applicable) 2. Open and close transactions in VR software 3. Conduct effective reference interview in face-to-face environment
Objectives:	At the completion of this training, you will be able to: 1. Interact with a single patron while searching a database or Web site 2. Identify common "Netspeak" abbreviations, such as hmt, idk, k, etc. 3. Formulate open questions 4. Formulate summaries and closed questions to confirm data requests 5. Apply strategies to identify key concepts in patron questions 6. Apply strategies to identify level of information needed by patrons 7. Apply strategies to identify for what purposes the information is to be used

Competency in Virtual Reference Encounter
or Interview: Intermediate Level

Effective virtual reference transactions depend on various elements working in concert. The virtual reference software, the availability of adequate resources, and the skill of the librarian conducting the reference interview are just some of the factors affecting the outcome of a reference transaction. Reference staff may demonstrate superior technical skills, for example, but still furnish incorrect answers to patrons. At the Intermediate level of competency for the virtual reference interview, LIS students and reference staff demonstrate increased comprehension of users' information-seeking needs and behavior and can increasingly apply that knowledge to their reference interviewing techniques. At this level, learners are expected to achieve the following skills and knowledge:

- understand the basic skills and theory behind user communication, interaction, and behavior and extend theory into practice
- ability to adapt to unexpected situations
- ability to assist users in applying critical thinking skills to searches

Below is a sample worksheet (Figure 9-14) outlining some virtual reference interview competencies at the Intermediate level. This worksheet can be

---

Figure 9-14: Sample Virtual Reference Encounter or Interview Worksheet—Intermediate Level

Goal:	To develop interviewing or encountering skills and knowledge consistent with the Intermediate level for virtual reference
Prerequisites:	Before participating in this training, you should be able to: 1. Interact with a single patron while searching database or Web site 2. Identify common "Netspeak" abbreviations, such as brb, idk, k, etc. 3. Apply strategies to identify key concepts in patron questions 4. Apply strategies to identify level of information needed by patrons
Objectives:	At the completion of this training, you will be able to: 1. Interact with two or more patrons while searching a database or Web site 2. Apply strategies to identify level of detail (i.e., raw data, or aggregate statistics?) 3. Devise ways to keep user(s) engaged as you search for information (questions, progress report, ask if they are searching, etc.) 4. Manage rude patrons in ways consistent with library policy

used as is or adapted for any virtual reference training program or LIS course in which virtual reference is taught. (Note: This worksheet is a general guide only and is meant to be used in conjunction with your own class and/or training content. It should be tailored to your specific needs and technologies.)

Competency in Virtual Reference Encounter or Interview: Advanced Level

The Advanced level of competency is characterized by a learner's ability to synthesize information effectively and to make assessments based on the information received. At this level, learners are expected to achieve the following skills and knowledge:

- ability to evaluate staff performance and their reference transactions
- ability to identify and implement procedures for improvement

Below is a sample worksheet (Figure 9-15) outlining some virtual reference interview competencies at the Advanced level. This worksheet can be used as is or can be adapted for any virtual reference training program or LIS course in which virtual reference is taught: (Note: This worksheet is a general guide only and is meant to be used in conjunction with your own class and/or training content. It should be tailored to your specific needs and technologies.)

Figure 9-15: Sample Virtual Reference Encounter or Interview Worksheet—Advanced Level	
Goal:	To develop interviewing or encountering skills and knowledge consistent with the Advanced level for virtual reference
Prerequisites:	Before participating in this training, you should be able to: 1. Interact with two or more patrons while searching a database or Web site 2. Apply strategies to identify a level of detail (i.e., raw data, or aggregate statistics?) 3. Devise ways to keep user(s) engaged as you search for information (questions, progress report, ask if they are searching, etc.) 4. Manage rude patrons in ways consistent with the library policy
Objectives:	At the completion of this training, you will be able to: 1. Identify components of effective and non-effective transactions through transcript analysis 2. Offer suggestions and solutions for more effective virtual interview and encounter techniques

Digital Information Resources Creation and Use

As digitized collections of information resources continue to grow, LIS students and reference staff often depend on high-quality digital resources to help them locate needed information. Ranging from images to historical documents, newspapers, journals, e-books, and many other items, the proliferation of digital information resources has been a great benefit to librarians providing virtual reference services.

In providing any type of reference service, reference staff members need to demonstrate a high level of competency in using library databases and other resources. With remote users expecting rapid responses to their questions, virtual reference providers should also possess superior searching skills for both Internet searches and in searching library databases. Learners' abilities to use Boolean logic, to deconstruct complex queries, and to demonstrate advanced problem-solving skills all dramatically increase as they progress through the three levels of competency.

In the DREI rubrics for virtual reference providers, competency in digital information resources creation and use focuses on practitioners' abilities to:

- demonstrate proficiency with library databases
- locate and use high-quality Web sites
- develop effective search strategies
- create new and useful digital resources
  (such as pathfinders)
- identify gaps in available resources

Competency in Digital Information Resources Creation and Use: Beginning Level

At the Beginning level of competency, the requirements focus on the attainment of the basic skills needed for providing virtual reference. For competency in digital information resources creation and use, the Beginning level concentrates on developing effective search strategies and the ability to select appropriate information resources available through the library.

By the end of the training or education program for the Beginning level, learners should be able to:

- construct and apply simple search strategies
- select most appropriate dataset from library's resources
- locate basic information using home library's resources (including online catalog and subscription databases)
- apply objective standards in evaluating information resources available through the library

The following sample worksheet (Figure 9-16) outlines some competencies for digital information resources creation and use at the Beginning level. This worksheet can be used as is or adapted for any virtual reference training program or LIS course in which virtual reference is taught. (Note: this worksheet is a general guide only and is meant to be used in conjunction with your

Figure 9-16: Sample Digital Information Resources Creation and Use Worksheet—Beginning Level

Goal:	To develop skills and knowledge regarding digital information resources creation and use consistent with the Beginning level for virtual reference
Prerequisites:	Before participating in this training, you should be able to: 1. Navigate library databases, VR software, and/or course management system (if applicable) 2. Manage two or more open application windows 3. Organize files in directories
Objectives:	At the completion of this training, you will be able to: 1. Select appropriate keywords for searches 2. Use basic Boolean operators 3. Locate basic information on the Web using search engines 4. Illustrate specific searches for users in a one-on-one interaction

own class and/or training content. It should be tailored to your specific needs and technologies.)

Competency in Digital Information Resources Creation and Use: Intermediate Level

The Intermediate level of competency in digital information resources creation and use requires learners to develop an increased awareness of both the resources used and the types of searches used to locate information. At this level, reference staff and LIS students are expected to use advanced Boolean operators, employ a variety of Web search engines and library databases, and begin to assess the quality of various information resources.

By the end of the training or education program for the Intermediate level, learners should be able to:

- construct and apply complex search strategies
- select most appropriate database from the library's resources and recommend resources available in other libraries
- understand the structure of literatures and answer complex queries using a variety of sources
- perform advanced searches using Web-based search engines
- conduct searches based on knowledge of Web-based directories and collections
- apply objective standards in evaluating information resources

The following sample worksheet (Figure 9-17) outlines some competencies for digital information resources creation and use at the Intermediate

Figure 9-17: Sample Digital Information Resources Creation and Use Worksheet—Intermediate Level

Goal:	To develop skills and knowledge regarding digital information resources creation and use consistent with the Intermediate level for virtual reference
Prerequisites:	Before participating in this training, you should be able to: 1. Navigate library databases, VR software, and/or course management system (if applicable) 2. Select appropriate keywords for searches 3. Use basic Boolean operators 4. Locate basic information on the Web using search engines 5. Illustrate specific searches for users in a one-on-one interaction
Objectives:	At the completion of this training, you will be able to: 1. Select appropriate keywords and subject headings 2. Use advanced Boolean operators 3. Understand and use advanced features of digital information sources 4. Compare appropriate resources 5. Judge appropriateness of resources for library's patrons 6. Recommend library acquisitions 7. Provide information literacy instruction to groups of users and colleagues 8. Create tools to facilitate user access to information resources

level. This worksheet can be used as is or can be adapted for any virtual reference training program or LIS course in which virtual reference is taught. (Note: This worksheet is a general guide only and is meant to be used in conjunction with your own class and/or training content. It should be tailored to your specific needs and technologies.)

Competency in Digital Information Resources
Creation and Use: Advanced Level
The ability to create new information resources to better serve an organization's user population is an important component in providing effective library service. At the Advanced level for competency in digital information resources creation and use, reference staff and LIS students are expected to create information products and resources to aid patrons, demonstrate superior search capabilities on a variety of databases and Web search engines, evaluate the quality and appropriateness of internal and external resources, and provide resource instruction to co-workers and patrons alike.

By the end of the training or education program for the Advanced level, learners should be able to:

- conduct searches based on knowledge of Web-based directories and collections
- work collaboratively to implement or create systems that facilitate access to information sources
- create new information products
- evaluate information resources on a system level

Below is a sample worksheet (Figure 9-18) outlining some competencies for digital information resources creation and use at the Advanced level. This worksheet can be used as is or can be adapted for any virtual reference training

---

Figure 9-18: Sample Digital Information Resources Creation and Use Worksheet—Advanced Level

Goal:	To develop skills and knowledge regarding digital information resources creation and use consistent with the Advanced level for virtual reference
Prerequisites:	Before participating in this training, you should be able to: 1. Select appropriate keywords and subject headings 2. Use advanced Boolean operators 3. Understand and use advanced features of digital information sources 4. Compare appropriate resources 5. Judge appropriateness of resources for library's patrons 6. Recommend library acquisitions 7. Provide information literacy instruction to groups of users and colleagues 8. Create tools to facilitate user access to information resources
Objectives:	At the completion of this training, you will be able to: 1. Construct and apply complex search strategies 2. Perform advanced searches using a variety of Web search engines 3. Navigate the invisible Web 4. Recommend and approve reference acquisitions 5. Provide information literacy instruction to groups of users and colleagues 6. Conduct advanced training program on information resources for reference staff

program or LIS course in which virtual reference is taught. (Note: This worksheet is a general guide only and is meant to be used in conjunction with your own class and/or training content. It should be tailored to your specific needs and technologies.)

Evaluation of Services

Evaluation is an often overlooked and sometimes unwelcome aspect of many libraries' services. Assessments can be time-consuming and expensive to conduct and may detract from other duties. Yet evaluation is vitally important to the successful operation of a virtual reference service, particularly as technology changes and users grow increasingly demanding in their information needs. Without periodic evaluation, a service is unable to determine whether it is actually meeting its goals, adhering to its policies, or making the best use of its available resources. Moreover, regular ongoing evaluation of virtual reference services allows administrators to examine staffing and training needs, the economic costs of providing such services, and the service's effect on the local reference department, the organization, and any partnering institutions (Wasik, 2003).

In the DREI rubrics for virtual reference providers, the evaluation of services competency focuses on practitioners' abilities to effectively assess:

- individual and aggregate virtual reference transactions
- effectiveness of the triage system
- user feedback
- timeliness of service responses

The assessment of these features, among others, helps ensure efficiency, quality, and reliability of virtual reference services.

Competency in Evaluation of Services: Beginning Level

At the Beginning level of competency in the evaluation of services, the focus is on the learner's self-assessment of their individual performance as it relates to virtual reference. While such an assessment can be conducted formally through surveys or questionnaires, self-assessment at this level also can be handled informally through discussions or one-on-one encounters with an administrator or instructor. Self-assessment is important because it helps learners identify their respective strengths, weaknesses, and skills that need to be improved.

The following is a sample worksheet (Figure 9-19) outlining some competencies for evaluation of services at the Beginning level. This worksheet can be used as is or adapted for any virtual reference training program or LIS course in which virtual reference is taught. (Note: This worksheet is a general guide only and is meant to be used in conjunction with your own class or training content. It should be tailored to your specific needs and technologies.)

Figure 9-19: Sample Evaluation of Services Worksheet— Beginning Level	
Goal:	To develop skills and knowledge in the evaluation of services consistent with the Beginning level for virtual reference
Prerequisites:	Before participating in this training, you should be able to: 1. Understand conceptually the structure and function of the service as it relates to the organization and community 2. Understand local virtual reference service policies and procedures
Objectives:	At the completion of this training, you will be able to: 1. Reflect on personal service given 2. Evaluate effectiveness of participation in library reference services 3. Identify areas for improvement

Competency in Evaluation of Services: Intermediate Level

At the Intermediate level, participants are asked to look critically beyond their own performance to that of their virtual reference service department as a whole. By the end of the training or education program, learners at this level should be able to contribute to the process of service evaluation by:

- reviewing department reference transcripts
- collecting user feedback through a variety of print and online methods
- noting any user feedback culled through informal means (personal conversation, etc.)

User feedback is perhaps one of the most valuable assessment tools for any library service and is particularly important in virtual services where visual cues are lacking to help gauge success. Regular review of departmental reference transcripts also helps note trends, recurring problems, or successful methods used in remote information provision. All of this information helps virtual reference services identify when they are meeting their goals and objectives and if improvements need to be made.

The following is a sample worksheet (Figure 9-20) outlining some competencies for evaluation of services at the Intermediate level. This worksheet can be used as is or adapted for any virtual reference training program or LIS course in which virtual reference is taught. (Note: This worksheet is a general guide only and is meant to be used in conjunction with your own class or training content. It should be tailored to your specific needs and technologies.)

Figure 9-20: Sample Evaluation of Services Worksheet— Intermediate Level

Goal:	To develop skills and knowledge in the evaluation of services consistent with the Intermediate level for virtual reference
Prerequisites:	Before participating in this training, you should be able to: 1. Reflect on personal service given 2. Evaluate effectiveness of participation in library reference services 3. Identify areas for improvement
Objectives:	At the completion of this training, you will be able to: 1. Demonstrate ability to effectively evaluate reference services 2. Participate in data collection for the library

Competency in Evaluation of Services: Advanced Level

The Advanced level of competency in the evaluation of services is characterized by a higher level of knowledge of the assessment process and understanding of how such assessments can be conducted and applied to services beyond the local organization. At this level, learners should be able to:

- analyze data collected through various types of assessment methods and make changes accordingly
- evaluate local service performance as both a standalone service and within a collaborative context
- oversee service evaluation projects

The following is a sample worksheet (Figure 9-21) outlining some competencies for evaluation of services at the Advanced level. This worksheet can be used as is or adapted for any virtual reference training program or LIS course in which virtual reference is taught. (Note: This worksheet is a

Figure 9-21: Sample Evaluation of Services Worksheet— Advanced Level

Goal:	To develop skills and knowledge in the evaluation of services consistent with the Advanced level for virtual reference
Prerequisites:	Before participating in this training, you should be able to: 1. Demonstrate the ability to evaluate reference services 2. Participate in data collection for the library
	(Cont'd.)

Figure 9-21: Sample Evaluation of Services Worksheet— Advanced Level *(Continued)*	
Objectives:	At the completion of this training, you will be able to: 1. Manage and implement evaluation projects 2. Implement changes based on evaluation project 3. Reflect on effectiveness of service provision within a collaborative environment 4. Correctly interpret data collected on reference services within the library

general guide only and is meant to be used in conjunction with your own class or training content. It should be tailored to your specific needs and technologies.)

Policies and Procedures

The advent of virtual reference has caused many libraries to re-evaluate their existing library and reference policies. Online reference transactions captured in transcripts, knowledge bases, or e-mail have raised questions about patron privacy and measures needed to protect it. Unlike traditional face-to-face reference encounters, virtual reference services can unwittingly attract a patron base that extends far beyond their intended user communities. Reference departments, then, need to consider many factors in drafting new policies regarding their virtual reference services. Some factors to consider include:

- User community: Local community, or the world at large?
- Question turnaround time: How long will responses take to reach a user if e-mail is used or if a chat transaction cannot be completed in the allotted time?
- The use of licensed databases to answer questions.
- Level of service: Will your service respond to homework questions, for example?
- Question limitations: Will patrons be allowed a certain number of questions within a specified timeframe?
- Inappropriate patron behavior.
- Confidentiality.

It is important to note that a service's policy and procedures will need periodic revision as the service evolves. Adaptation of existing policy and procedures maintains the standards and professionalism of the service and safeguards the library and its staff in disputes regarding service or staff performance. It is also important that all virtual reference service policies reflect the organization's overall mission and objectives.

Competency in Policies and Procedures: Beginning Level
At the Beginning level of competency in policies and procedures for virtual reference, training should focus on the participants' knowledge of the service's policies and understanding of how these policies are used to establish factors such as level of service, limits to the service, and its priorities.

By the end of the training or education program for the Beginning level, learners should be able to:

- understand and explain the institution's policy and procedural guidelines
- understand and explain the policy and procedures for collaborative service with partner organizations (if applicable)

Below is a sample worksheet (Figure 9-22) outlining some competencies for policy and procedures at the Beginning level. This worksheet can be used as is or adapted for any virtual reference training program or LIS course in which virtual reference is taught. (Note: This worksheet is a general guide only and is meant to be used in conjunction with your own class or training content. It should be tailored to your specific needs and technologies.)

Figure 9-22: Sample Policies and Procedures Worksheet—Beginning Level	
Goal:	To develop skills and knowledge in policy and procedures consistent with the Beginning level for virtual reference
Prerequisites:	Before participating in this training, you should be able to: 1. Locate written policy and procedures for both the institution and the virtual reference service

Objectives:	At the completion of this training, you will be able to:
	
	1. Understand and explain the institution's policy and procedural guidelines for:
	  a. scope of service f. privacy
	  b. triage g. transaction length
	  c. question referral (chat reference)
	  d. declining questions h. document delivery
	  e. turnaround time i. patron misbehavior
	
	2. Understand and explain policy and procedures for collaborative service with partner institutions (if applicable) for:
	  a. scope of service f. transaction length
	  b. triage (chat reference)
	  c. question referral g. document delivery
	  d. turnaround time h. hours of service
	  e. privacy i. patron misbehavior

Competency in Policy and Procedures: Intermediate Level
At the Intermediate level of competency in policy and procedures, training and education participants look more broadly at virtual reference policy. Many organizations are involved in collaborative reference efforts, and policy for consortial reference may differ from the institution's local policy and procedures. For example, different services partnered in a collaborative effort may have different levels of service. Such differences must be worked out and a common policy agreed to if a high level of service for users of the combined service is to be maintained. The Intermediate level of competency in policy and procedures features a more detailed understanding of the components of good policy and procedures, and how good policy produces effective procedure.

Below is a sample worksheet (Figure 9-23) outlining some competencies for policy and procedures at the Intermediate level. This worksheet can be used as is or adapted for any virtual reference training program or LIS course in which virtual reference is taught. (Note: This worksheet is a general guide only and is meant to be used in conjunction with your own class or training content. It should be tailored to your specific needs and technologies.)

Competency in Policy and Procedures: Advanced Level
At the Advanced level of competency for virtual reference policy and procedures, learners should be able to contribute actively to the creation of new policy and procedures on both local and consortial levels. By this stage, learners can appraise existing policy and procedures for gaps, discrepancies, or irrelevant information and make revisions accordingly.

Figure 9-23: Sample Policies and Procedures Worksheet—Intermediate Level	
Goal:	To develop skills and knowledge in policy and procedures consistent with the Intermediate level for virtual reference
Prerequisites:	Before participating in this training, you should be able to: 1. Understand the institution's policy and procedural guidelines (i.e., triage, question referral, declining questions, etc.) 2. Understand and explain policy and procedures for collaborative service with partner institutions (if applicable)
Objectives:	At the completion of this training, you will be able to: 1. Understand more broadly the virtual reference policy across institutions 2. Identify features that comprise good policy 3. Evaluate procedures in light of policy

Figure 9-24: Sample Policies and Procedures Worksheet—Advanced Level	
Goal:	To develop skills and knowledge in policy and procedures consistent with the Advanced level for virtual reference
Prerequisites:	Before participating in this training, you should be able to: 1. Understand more broadly about virtual reference policy across institutions 2. Identify features that make good policy 3. Evaluate procedures in light of policy
Objectives:	At the completion of this training, you will be able to: 1. Craft and implement widescale institutional policy and procedures for virtual reference 2. Evaluate policy to ensure it complies with existing laws

The sample worksheet above (Figure 9-24) outlines some competencies for policy and procedures at the Advanced level. This worksheet can be used as is or adapted for any virtual reference training program or LIS course in which virtual reference is taught. Note: This worksheet is a general guide only and is meant to be used in conjunction with your own class or training content. It should be tailored to your specific needs and technologies.)

Instructional Role

Virtual reference services offer many different levels of service according to their missions and resources. Academic libraries traditionally have sought to include information literacy instruction in their transactions with in-person patrons and largely have tried to continue this practice in the virtual environment. Many public and special libraries also attempt to provide instruction in their reference transactions. While some libraries and other organizations conduct formal information literacy skills instruction in the way of classes or workshops, much instruction is conducted informally in everyday transactions. Examples of informal reference instruction may include providing:

- search tips and suggestions
- suggestions for appropriate databases (and why)
- effective keyword searches for Web search engines
- instruction in the use of OPAC
- instruction in reading a bibliographic record

Instruction, however, is not limited exclusively to patrons. The instructional role competency as outlined in the DREI guidelines consists of two types of instruction:

- educating users in order to enhance their information literacy skills
- training staff in virtual reference skills

All reference staff should be able to instruct both patrons and colleagues in learning new skills and tools. As staff members progress through the outlined levels of competency, they can provide more in-depth instruction for both co-workers and patrons alike.

Competency in Instructional Role: Beginning Level
The instructional role competency at the Beginning level concentrates on learners' abilities to convey information to others in a logical and consistent fashion. While many LIS students and reference staff members may demonstrate proficiency in searching databases or using the local virtual reference software, achieving the instructional role competency at the Beginning level requires additional skills. Reference practitioners, for example, must learn how to subtly introduce instructional elements into their dealings with patrons, as well as show new colleagues the basics of navigating the virtual reference software.

By the end of the training or education program for the Beginning level, learners should be able to:

- integrate instruction in the basics of searching the library's OPAC, databases, and Web sites into virtual reference encounters
- teach colleagues how to perform basic operations in the virtual reference software package/system

Below is a sample worksheet (Figure 9-25) outlining some competencies in instructional role at the Beginning level. This worksheet can be used as is or adapted for any virtual reference training program or LIS course in which virtual reference is taught. (Note: This worksheet is a general guide only and is meant to be used in conjunction with your own class or training content. It should be tailored to your specific needs and technologies.)

Figure 9-25: Sample Instructional Role Worksheet— Beginning Level

Goal:	To develop instructional skills and knowledge consistent with the Beginning level for virtual reference
Prerequisites:	Before participating in this training, you should be able to: 1. Perform basic searches using library databases and Internet search engines 2. Demonstrate competency in local virtual reference software at the Intermediate or Advanced level

(Cont'd.)

	Figure 9-25: Sample Instructional Role Worksheet—Beginning Level *(Continued)*	

Objectives:	At the completion of this training, you will be able to:
	
	1. Integrate instruction in the basics of searching the library OPAC, databases, and Web sites into virtual reference encounters, such as:
	  a. selection of appropriate keywords for searches
	  b. basic Boolean operators to refine searches
	  c. appropriate database selection
	  d. basic subject heading instruction
	
	2. Teach staff members how to perform basic operations of the virtual reference software, such as:
	  a. Log in and out of a selected VR software package
	  b. Open a virtual reference query
	  c. Navigate various features in the VR software
	  d. Use canned messages appropriately
	  e. Successfully engage and respond to patron inquiries via VR package (single patron at a time)
	  f. Transfer questions to another operator or level in the consortial network
	  g. End a transaction in the software	

Competency in Instructional Role: Intermediate Level

The instructional role competency at the Intermediate level focuses on a learner's abilities to think critically about information choices and how to articulate these choices to users. The ability to explain why certain resources are appropriate for various information needs is a critical component in teaching information literacy skills. As reference staff members give their reasons for selecting certain resources over others, users can begin to apply their own critical thinking skills to their individual information needs. In this way, reference staff members teach users how to make informed choices about the types of resources that best meet the latter's needs.

Below is a sample worksheet (Figure 9-26) outlining some competencies in the instructional role at the Intermediate level. This worksheet can be used as is or adapted for any virtual reference training program or LIS course in

	Figure 9-26: Sample Instructional Role Worksheet—Intermediate Level	
Goal:	To develop instructional skills and knowledge consistent with the Intermediate level for virtual reference	
		(Cont'd.)

Figure 9-26: Sample Instructional Role Worksheet— Intermediate Level *(Continued)*	
Prerequisites:	Before participating in this training, you should be able to: 1. Integrate instruction in the basics of searching the library OPAC, databases, and Web sites into virtual reference encounters 2. Teach staff members how to perform basic operations using the virtual reference software
Objectives:	At the completion of this training, you will be able to: 1. Promote information literacy by assisting users in applying critical thinking skills to locating and evaluating information during virtual reference encounters 2. Develop virtual reference instructional units for users and user groups based on task/need 3. Teach staff members how to integrate virtual reference into reference services and determine when and why to use it

which virtual reference is taught. (Note: This worksheet is a general guide only and is meant to be used in conjunction with your own class or training content. It should be tailored to your specific needs and technologies.)

Competency in Instructional Role: Advanced Level
The Advanced level of competency focuses on the participants' abilities to apply higher-level planning and critical thinking skills to the role of instruction in virtual reference transactions. At this level, participants understand the value of instruction in virtual reference encounters and think continuously about how best to incorporate instructional practices into reference service.

Below is a sample worksheet (Figure 9-27) outlining some competencies in instructional role at the Advanced level. This worksheet can be used as is or adapted for any virtual reference training program or LIS course in which virtual reference is taught. (Note: This worksheet is a general guide only and is meant to be used in conjunction with your own class or training content. It should be tailored to your specific needs and technologies.)

Figure 9-27: Sample Instructional Role Worksheet— Advanced Level	
Goal:	To develop instructional skills and knowledge consistent with the Advanced level for virtual reference
	(Cont'd.)

	Figure 9-27: Sample Instructional Role Worksheet—Advanced Level (*Continued*)
Prerequisites:	Before participating in this training, you should be able to:
	1. Promote information literacy by assisting users in applying critical thinking skills in locating and evaluating information during virtual reference encounters
	2. Develop virtual reference instructional units for users and user groups based on task/need
	3. Teach staff members how to integrate virtual reference into reference services and determine when and why to use it
Objectives:	At the completion of this training, you will be able to develop:
	1. Policy to guide integration of instruction by staff into virtual reference encounters
	2. Curriculum and infrastructure that supports training of staff
	3. Curriculum that addresses needs determined by evaluating librarian transcripts, i.e., knowledge base acquisition

Triage and Collaboration

As the number of virtual reference transactions continues to rise, libraries must periodically reevaluate their staffing levels and assignments. Organizations that add virtual services without hiring additional staff often find that their staff members become overtaxed due to the increased demands. Unfortunately, it is still not uncommon to find some librarians attempting to provide in-person, telephone, and virtual reference services simultaneously. The results of such overburdening of staff can lead to a lower level of service to patrons and reduced staff morale.

To help manage large question loads and provide extended services to their patrons, many libraries have developed partnerships with other libraries, either nationally or internationally. A library in New York, for example, may partner with a library in California to share services, with the East Coast library providing morning reference services and the West Coast library providing them in the evening. While the transactions are generally seamless to patrons, each library is able to extend their hours of operation without hiring additional staff or overburdening the existing one. Where operating budgets allow, some organizations also have turned to staffing services to outsource questions during off-hours or to help supplement limited staff.

Triage, or the process of assigning and routing reference questions from remote patrons, is a critical component in the operation of virtual reference services. Questions may be routed internally to various librarians or subject experts or externally to other services. At a minimum, reference practitioners and LIS students must identify the general subject area that a reference question addresses and route or assign the question to an appropriate subject expert or service. While triage may be relatively straightforward in one organization, collaborative virtual reference services each may have their own individual triage policies and methods. In such cases, the services should create and adopt a single method of triage when routing questions among collaborating services to maintain a consistent level of service and prevent misunderstandings between services.

In the DREI rubrics for virtual reference providers, competency in triage and collaboration focuses on a practitioner's ability to:

- assess user information needs
- make appropriate referrals to other services and/or organizations
- identify and create effective policies and procedures
- evaluate collaborative efforts

Whether reference services are provided in-house, across a continent, or from a librarian's home, reference staff must be able to understand the triage system both at their local organization's level and at a collaborative level.

Competency in Triage and Collaboration: Beginning Level

This level is characterized by participants assessing user information needs effectively. One of the most fundamental aspects of triage is assigning at least a general subject heading to a question. In some cases, this may be challenging. It is not uncommon for users, especially when submitting questions via e-mail or Web forms, to submit multiple questions within one transaction. The challenge here is for reference staff to assign a question to the appropriate subject expert (if applicable) and designate a subject area to a multiple-part question.

Below is a sample worksheet (Figure 9-28) outlining competencies in triage and collaboration at the Beginning level. This worksheet can be used as is or adapted for any virtual reference training program or LIS course in which virtual reference is taught. (Note: This worksheet is a general guide only and is

---

Figure 9-28: Sample Triage and Collaboration Worksheet— Beginning Level

Goal:	To develop skills and knowledge in triage and collaboration consistent with the Beginning level for virtual reference
Prerequisites:	Before participating in this training, you should be able to: 1. Perform basic operations within the virtual reference software and understand the functions of each operation 2. Understand the institution's policy and procedural guidelines (i.e., triage, question referral, declining questions, etc.)

(Cont'd.)

Figure 9-28: Sample Triage and Collaboration Worksheet—Beginning Level *(Continued)*

Objectives:	At the completion of this training, you will be able to: 1. Apply subject headings to questions 2. Write brief descriptions of questions 3. Apply appropriate metadata 4. Successfully route questions with all the required information 5. Follow specified policies and procedures for collaborative conduct

meant to be used in conjunction with your own class or training content. It should be tailored to your specific needs and technologies.)

Competency in Triage and Collaboration: Intermediate Level

At this level, LIS students and reference staff members can make higher-level triage and collaboration decisions. With a fuller understanding of partner institutions' relative strengths, weaknesses, availability, and resources, learners at this level can route questions both in- and out-of-house to appropriate experts more accurately than at the Beginning level of competency. Training participants at the Intermediate level also become increasingly adept at dissecting questions for unexpressed information requests. Children, for example, often unintentionally ask one thing when they actually mean something different. With sometimes limited vocabularies and experience, it is not uncommon for children or other users (such as those for whom English is not their native language) to include misspellings or inaccurate information in their requests. Successful triage depends on reference staff members and LIS students becoming attuned to the nuances of digital questions and locating the best information or human resources to answer them.

Below is a sample worksheet (Figure 9-29) outlining competencies in triage and collaboration at the Intermediate level. This worksheet can be used as is or adapted for any virtual reference training program or LIS course in

Figure 9-29: Sample Triage and Collaboration Worksheet—Intermediate Level

Goal:	To develop skills and knowledge in triage and collaboration consistent with the Intermediate level for virtual reference

(Cont'd.)

Figure 9-29: Sample Triage and Collaboration Worksheet—Intermediate Level (Continued)	
Prerequisites:	Before participating in this training, you should be able to: 1. Apply subject headings to questions 2. Write brief descriptions of questions 3. Apply appropriate metadata 4. Successfully route questions with all the required information 5. Follow specified policies and procedures for collaborative conduct
Objectives:	At the completion of this training, you will be able to: 1. Recognize questions that are suitable for referral 2. Apply appropriate criteria in selecting among multiple referral options 3. Understand the strengths and weaknesses of collaborative partners 4. Recognize question types and contextual factors that affect question handling 5. Recognize underlying and unexpressed information needs

which virtual reference is taught. (Note: This worksheet is a general guide only and is meant to be used in conjunction with your own class or training content. It should be tailored to your specific needs and technologies.

Competency in Triage and Collaboration: Advanced Level
The Advanced level is characterized by a participant's ability to lead collaborative efforts and set triage and collaboration policies. At this stage in the training or education program, learners can assume more administrative duties associated with triage and collaboration, such as:

- Schedule virtual reference service coverage with partner institutions
- Evaluate effectiveness of triage efforts for local organization and collaborative partners
- Identify and develop additional collaborative partnerships

The following is a sample worksheet (Figure 9-30) outlining competencies in triage and collaboration at the Advanced level. This worksheet can be used as is or adapted for any virtual reference training program or LIS course in which virtual reference is taught. (Note: This worksheet is a general guide only and is meant to be used in conjunction with your own class or training content. It should be tailored to your specific needs and technologies.

Figure 9-30: Sample Triage and Collaboration Worksheet—Advanced Level	
Goal:	To develop skills and knowledge in triage and collaboration consistent with the Advanced level for virtual reference
Prerequisites:	Before participating in this training, you should be able to: 1. Apply subject headings to questions 2. Write brief descriptions of questions 3. Apply appropriate metadata 4. Successfully route questions with all the required information 5. Follow specified policies and procedures for collaborative conduct
Objectives:	At the completion of this training, you will be able to: 1. Follow up to ensure that referred questions are answered 2. Work interactively with collaborators to schedule coverage and provide training 3. Assess effectiveness of collaborative efforts 4. Make policy decisions regarding triage and collaboration 5. Identify and pursue new opportunities for collaboration

Virtual Reference Community

The virtual reference community has expanded considerably in the last decade. Beginning with a handful of library services in the early 1990s, there are now thousands of services offered by a range of nonprofit and commercial organizations. One of the hallmarks of virtual reference providers has been their willingness to share ideas, resources, and experiences with other current or would-be services. This climate of openness and generosity has helped spur the rapid growth of virtual reference services and led to tremendous technological advances in how the information community provides services.

The DREI competencies for virtual reference community feature two distinct types of applications for reference practitioners and LIS students:

- Internal: Understanding the value of continuing education.
- External: Appreciation of the wider community of virtual reference services.

Reference practitioners and LIS students contribute to their personal development and their institutions by their commitment to participating in professional development and continuing education opportunities. They also may contribute to the wider virtual reference community by participating in online discussions, conferences, meetings, and other events. The effect of such participation, on both internal and external levels, advances the virtual reference agenda and virtual services for patrons worldwide.

Competency in Virtual Reference Community: Beginning Level

The Beginning level of competency in virtual reference community focuses on a learner's growing recognition of virtual reference efforts outside of the local service. The awareness of other services offers participants an opportunity to learn about the policies, technologies, challenges, and initiatives at other virtual reference services and how such efforts compare with their own.

Below is a sample worksheet (Figure 9-31) outlining competencies in virtual reference community at the Beginning level. This worksheet can be used as is or adapted for any virtual reference training program or LIS course in which virtual reference is taught. (Note: This worksheet is a general guide only and is meant to be used in conjunction with your own class or training content. It should be tailored to your specific needs and technologies.)

Competency in Virtual Reference Community: Intermediate Level

At the Intermediate level, participants understand the value of continuing education as an agent for change in the virtual reference community. While the Beginning level features a growing awareness of virtual reference services apart from participants' local services, the Intermediate level is characterized by the learners' outreach and growing participation in virtual reference discussions and events.

Figure 9-31: Sample Virtual Reference Community Worksheet— Beginning Level	
Goal:	To develop the skills and knowledge necessary to contribute to the virtual reference community consistent with the Beginning level for virtual reference
Prerequisites:	Before participating in this training, you should be able to: 1. Understand the benefits of continuing education and professional development opportunities on a personal and organizational level 2. Use Web search engines to locate information on virtual reference services locally and nationally
Objectives:	At the completion of this training, you will be able to: 1. Seek opportunities for continuing education 2. Develop knowledge of wider virtual reference community through listservs, organizations, conferences, and networking

Figure 9-32: Sample Virtual Reference Community Worksheet—Intermediate Level	
Goal:	To develop the skills and knowledge necessary to contribute to the virtual reference community consistent with the Intermediate level for virtual reference
Prerequisites:	Before participating in this training, you should be able to: 1. Seek opportunities for continuing education 2. Develop knowledge of wider virtual reference community through listservs, organizations, conferences, and networking
Objectives:	At the completion of this training, you will be able to: 1. Contribute to the growth of the virtual reference field through participation in actual and virtual forums 2. Understand how the wider community affects the local institution 3. Recommend new and different ways of approaching virtual reference problems and concerns

The sample worksheet above (Figure 9-32) outlines competencies in virtual reference community at the Intermediate level. This worksheet can be used as is or adapted for any virtual reference training program or LIS course in which virtual reference is taught. (Note: This worksheet is a general guide only and is meant to be used in conjunction with your own class or training content. It should be tailored to your specific needs and technologies.)

Competency in Virtual Reference Community: Advanced Level

At this level, participants provide encouragement and opportunities for continuing education for reference staff members and LIS students. Learners achieving the Advanced level of competency in virtual reference community realize that ongoing education and participation in various types of virtual reference forums by all staff members benefits the overall service.

The following is a sample worksheet (Figure 9-33) outlining competencies in virtual reference community at the Advanced level. This worksheet can be used as is or adapted for any virtual reference training program or LIS course in which virtual reference is taught. (Note: This worksheet is a general guide only and is meant to be used in conjunction with your own class or training content. It should be tailored to your specific needs and technologies.

Knowledge Base Acquisition and Use

As the number of virtual reference transactions increases at many libraries, reference staff members often see a high number of repeat questions. Rather than

Figure 9-33: Sample Virtual Reference Community Worksheet—Advanced Level	
Goal:	To develop the skills and knowledge necessary to contribute to the virtual reference community consistent with the Advanced level for virtual reference
Prerequisites:	Before participating in this training, you should be able to: 1. Contribute to the growth of the virtual reference field through participation in actual and virtual forums 2. Understand how the wider community affects the local institution 3. Recommend new and different ways of approaching virtual reference problems and concerns
Objectives:	At the completion of this training, you will be able to: 1. Actively support virtual reference collaborative efforts within and outside the institution 2. Contribute to the wider virtual reference community through publications and presentations 3. Implement new ways of solving problems and making the library a good place to work

research and write a new response to the same question each time, librarians have sought to capture the information so that it could be re-used in future transactions. In the early days of virtual reference, many reference departments created frequently-asked question (FAQ) Web pages or kept an archive of previously asked-and-answered question sets. While such resources are helpful, they often are difficult to search quickly. As a result, many reference practitioners have discovered the benefits of using knowledge bases to capture their reference transactions. Although there are different types of "data warehouses," knowledge bases generally are recognized as centralized repositories of information. Reference staff members may, for example, use a database product to record reference transactions. This way, relevant data may be located with keyword searches and/or under subject headings. It is important to note that effective knowledge bases are not static resources. Content must be reviewed periodically and updated to keep it current.

There are several benefits to using knowledge bases to capture reference transactions, including:

- Faster service to patrons—answers found in the knowledge base reduce transaction length and free reference staff members to help other patrons.
- Knowledge retention—the knowledge accumulated by seasoned reference staff is often difficult to replicate or replace. In the case of a longtime

staff member's retirement or job change, the remaining staff members can be left scrambling to re-create the knowledge lost after his or her departure. Knowledge bases can help ensure that specific knowledge is captured and retained within the organization.

- Improved patron satisfaction—patrons want their information as quickly as possible. Providing high-quality information rapidly is always appreciated by users, and the use of knowledge bases can help support these efforts.

Competency in Knowledge Base Acquisition and Use: Beginning Level

At the Beginning level of competency in knowledge base acquisition and use, learners focus on understanding the fundamental concepts of knowledge bases and becoming proficient in using them.

Below is a sample worksheet (Figure 9-34) outlining competencies in knowledge base acquisition and use at the Beginning level. This worksheet can be used as is or adapted for any virtual reference training program or LIS course in which virtual reference is taught. (Note: This worksheet is a general guide only and is meant to be used in conjunction with your own class or training content. It should be tailored to your specific needs and technologies.)

Competency in Knowledge Base Acquisition and Use: Intermediate Level

At the Intermediate level of competency in knowledge base acquisition and use, LIS students and reference staff members demonstrate increased comprehension of knowledge base functions and can evaluate such functions and

Figure 9-34: Sample Knowledge Base Acquisition and Use Worksheet—Beginning Level

Goal:	To develop skills and knowledge in knowledge base acquisition and use consistent with the Beginning level for virtual reference
Prerequisites:	Before participating in this training, you should be able to: 1. Successfully navigate database software or commercial knowledge base software 2. Use appropriate keywords for searches
Objectives:	At the completion of this training, you will be able to: 1. Recognize resources created by colleagues through databases of questions and answers 2. Use the resources created by colleagues

Figure 9-35: Sample Knowledge Base Acquisition and Use Worksheet—Intermediate Level

Goal:	To develop skills and knowledge in knowledge base acquisition and use consistent with the Intermediate level for virtual reference
Prerequisites:	Before participating in this training, you should be able to: 1. Recognize resources created by colleagues through databases of questions and answers 2. Use the resources created by colleagues
Objectives:	At the completion of this training, you will be able to: 1. Evaluate the appropriateness and efficacy of knowledge base resources 2. Demonstrate awareness of and provide feedback on policy governing knowledge base acquisition and use

their appropriateness to their organization. As their understanding of the strengths and shortcomings of the knowledge base increases, learners also contribute to knowledge base policy and use.

The sample worksheet above (Figure 9-35) outlines competencies in knowledge base acquisition and use at the Intermediate level. This worksheet can be used as is or adapted for any virtual reference training program or LIS course in which virtual reference is taught. (Note: This worksheet is a general guide only and is meant to be used in conjunction with your own class or training content. It should be tailored to your specific needs and technologies.)

Competency in Knowledge Base Acquisition and Use:
Advanced Level

At the Advanced level, learners demonstrate the ability to think critically about knowledge base functions and can apply this understanding to the refinement or creation of new knowledge base resources. They may find, for example, that subject-specific knowledge bases may be helpful to their organization, or that allowing patrons to search the library's knowledge base before submitting a question improves overall service efficiency.

The following sample worksheet (Figure 9-36) outlines competencies in knowledge base acquisition and use at the Advanced level. This worksheet can be used as is or adapted for any virtual reference training program or LIS course in which virtual reference is taught. (Note: This worksheet is a general guide only and is meant to be used in conjunction with your own class or training content. It should be tailored to your specific needs and technologies.)

Figure 9-36: Sample Knowledge Base Acquisition and Use Worksheet—Advanced Level

Goal:	To develop skills and knowledge in knowledge base acquisition and use consistent with the Advanced level for virtual reference
Prerequisites:	Before participating in this training, you should be able to: 1. Evaluate the appropriateness and efficacy of knowledge base resources 2. Demonstrate awareness of and provide feedback on policy governing knowledge base acquisition and use
Objectives:	At the completion of this training, you will be able to: 1. Plan and implement resource creation from data gathered from reference transactions 2. Interpret data from knowledge base and apply findings to library services 3. Use data mining techniques to refine or expand results

Appendix

Figure 9-37: Rubrics at a Glance

COMPETENCY	BEGINNING: *skills focus*	INTERMEDIATE: *conceptual focus*	ADVANCED: *administrative focus*
Computer Literacy • Ability to perform basic computer actions to facilitate digital reference encounters • Ability to be adaptable to different software requirements and platforms • Ability to formulate criteria and evaluate performance	Demonstrates the ability to do the following at a basic level required for job: • Login • Commands • Search operators • Upload • Protocols • Proxy • Download • Keyboarding skills	• Ability to perform basic computer actions at an appropriate level required for job • Ability to be adaptable to different software requirements and platforms	• Ability to perform basic computer actions at an appropriate level required for job • Ability to be adaptable to different software requirements and platforms • Ability to formulate specific competency criteria

(Cont'd.)

Figure 9-37: Rubrics at a Glance *(Continued)*

COMPETENCY	BEGINNING: *skills focus*	INTERMEDIATE: *conceptual focus*	ADVANCED: *administrative focus*
Computer Literacy *(Cont'd.)*	• Basic troubleshooting skills		• Ability to evaluate performance based on specific competency criteria
Digital Reference Software • Ability to use virtual reference software to facilitate digital reference encounters • Ability to formulate software criteria and make future recommendations	Demonstrates the ability to use one digital reference software program to answer patron inquiries: • Ability to log in and out of digital reference software • Ability to open and close a digital reference transaction • Ability to navigate software features, with an understanding of the functions of each feature • Ability to use canned messages • Recognize the difference between local and consortial applications, or aspects of these, in one software application	Possesses a higher level of understanding of features of a variety of digital reference software: • Recognizes similar features among different digital reference software • Knows how local and consortial portions of the software relate to each other • Understands and communicates which changes or additional features might be desirable in the digital reference software, and how such changes might improve service to users	Understands how software relates to other issues such as policy, communication, and service Possesses thorough knowledge of digital reference software in use at his/her institution, both locally and consortially (if applicable): • Ability to apply expertise to provide formal digital reference software training to other operators • Ability to write documentation for use of software under supervision of administrator • Understands relationship between local and consortial policies and the chosen software

(Cont'd.)

Figure 9-37: Rubrics at a Glance *(Continued)*			
COMPETENCY	BEGINNING: *skills focus*	INTERMEDIATE: *conceptual focus*	ADVANCED: *administrative focus*
Digital Reference Software *(Cont'd.)*	• Ability to transfer questions to another operator or level within a consortial network • Report digital software problems with adequate detail to an appropriate contact person	Possesses comprehensive knowledge of all operator features of one piece of the digital reference software: • Utilizes more complex software features such as co-browse and address books • Ability to manage multiple users in a queue Demonstrates facility with digital reference software: • Ability to easily adapt to changes to software in use at his/her institution • Provides preliminary triage for digital reference software problems before reporting to a contact person (both locally and consortially, if applicable) • Ability to assist other operators one-on-one with use of the digital reference software	Demonstrates basic understanding of administrative functions of digital reference software and can assist with administration when asked: • Uses canned reports to generate statistics • Ability to change passwords and add operators • Ability to install and configure digital reference software on operator's computers Applies conceptual knowledge of DR software to assist with the evaluation of software selection, as well as acquisition and implementation recommendations Keeps current on trends and developments in digital reference software
			(Cont'd)

Figure 9-37: Rubrics at a Glance *(Continued)*

COMPETENCY	BEGINNING: *skills focus*	INTERMEDIATE: *conceptual focus*	ADVANCED: *administrative focus*
Digital Reference Software *(Cont'd.)*		• Ability to change modes of communication for inquiries where appropriate, e.g., chat to e-mail	
Digital Reference Encountering or Interview • Information-seeking behavior • Ability to compensate for non-verbal cues • Elicitation techniques • Attention to politeness and proper virtual etiquette • Answer formulation and presentation • Relationship building	Understands at the level of Virtual Reference Desk instructions • Ability to follow basic procedures listed • Ability to adapt to unexpected situations • Ability to assist users in applying critical thinking to searches	Understands basics and theory behind user communication, interaction, and behavior • Ability to extend theory into practice • Ability to assist users in applying critical thinking to searches	• Ability to evaluate performance and transactions of staff • Identifies and implements procedures for improvement
Digital Information Resources Creation and Use • Library databases • Web sites • Searching strategies • Creation of new digital resources (i.e., pathfinders) • Identification of gaps in resources	Ability to construct and apply simple search strategies: • Can select appropriate keywords • Ability to use basic Boolean operators	Ability to construct and apply complex search strategies: • Ability to select appropriate keywords and subject headings	Ability to construct and apply complex search strategies Ability to select most appropriate database from library resources and recommend

(Cont'd.)

Figure 9-37: Rubrics at a Glance *(Continued)*

COMPETENCY	BEGINNING: *skills focus*	INTERMEDIATE: *conceptual focus*	ADVANCED: *administrative focus*
Digital Information Resources Creation and Use *(Cont'd.)*	Ability to select most appropriate dataset from library's resources Ability to find basic information using home library's resources, including online catalog and subscription databases Ability to locate basic information on the Web using search engines Ability to apply objective standards in evaluating information resources available through the library Ability to illustrate a specific search for users in a one-on-one interaction	• Ability to use advanced Boolean operators • Understands and is able to use advanced features of digital information sources Ability to select most appropriate database from library's resources, and can recommend resources available in other libraries Understands the structure of literatures, and answers complex inquiries using a variety of sources Ability to perform advanced searches using Web search engines Ability to conduct searches based on knowledge of directories and collections on the Web	resources available in other libraries Understands the structure of literatures and answers complex inquiries using a variety of sources Ability to perform advanced searches on Web search engines Ability to conduct searches based on knowledge of directories and collections on the Web Ability to navigate the invisible Web Ability to apply objective standards in evaluating information resources: • Ability to make recommendations and approve acquisitions • Ability to evaluate information resources on a system level

(Cont'd.)

Figure 9-37: Rubrics at a Glance *(Continued)*

COMPETENCY	BEGINNING: *skills focus*	INTERMEDIATE: *conceptual focus*	ADVANCED: *administrative focus*
Digital Information Resources Creation and Use *(Cont'd.)*		Ability to apply objective standards in evaluating information resources: • Can compare appropriate resources • Ability to judge appropriateness for library's patrons • Ability to make recommendations for acquisition • Ability to provide literacy instruction to groups of users and colleagues • Ability to create tools to facilitate user access to information resources	Ability to provide information literacy instruction to groups of users and colleagues Ability to conduct advanced training programs for reference staff Ability to create tools to facilitate user access to information resources Ability to create new information products Ability to work collaboratively to implement or create systems that facilitate access to information sources
Evaluation of Services • Effectiveness of triage • Individual and aggregate transactions • User feedback • Timeliness	• Ability to reflect on personal service given • Ability to evaluate effectiveness of participation in library reference services • Ability to identify areas for improvement	• Ability to effectively evaluate reference services • Participates in data collection for library	• Ability to manage and implement evaluation projects • Ability to implement changes based on an evaluation project

(Cont'd.)

Figure 9-37: **Rubrics at a Glance** *(Continued)*

COMPETENCY	BEGINNING: *skills focus*	INTERMEDIATE: *conceptual focus*	ADVANCED: *administrative focus*
Digital Information Resources Creation and Use *(Cont'd.)*			• Ability to reflect on effectiveness of service provision within the collaborative environment • Ability to correctly interpret data collected on reference services within the library
Policy and Procedures • Addresses both staff and user needs • Helps staff achieve learning goals	• Knows the institution's policy and procedural guidelines for triage, referral, declining inquiries, etc.	• Understands more broadly about digital reference policies across institutions • Ability to identify features to be included in effective policies • Ability to evaluate procedures in light of policies	• Ability to craft and implement wide-scale institutional policies and procedures for digital reference • Ability to evaluate policies and ensure that policies are in compliance with existing laws
Instructional Role • Educating users to enhance their information literacy • Training staff in digital reference skills	• Ability to integrate instruction in the basics of searching library's online catalog, databases, and Web sites into digital reference encounters	• Ability to promote information literacy by assisting users in applying critical thinking skills in locating and evaluating information during digital reference encounters	• Ability to develop policy to guide integration of instruction by staff into digital reference encounters • Ability to develop curriculum and infrastructure that supports staff training

(Cont'd.)

Figure 9-37: **Rubrics at a Glance** *(Continued)*

COMPETENCY	BEGINNING: *skills focus*	INTERMEDIATE: *conceptual focus*	ADVANCED: *administrative focus*
Instructional Role *(Cont'd.)*	• Ability to teach staff members how to perform basic operations of the digital reference software	• Ability to develop digital reference instructional units for users and user groups based on need or task • Ability to teach staff members how to effectively integrate digital reference into traditional refer-ence services (when and why to use it)	• Ability to develop curriculum and infrastructure that supports staff training • Ability to develop curriculum that addresses needs determined by evaluation of librarian transcripts, such as knowledge base acquisition
Triage and Collaboration • User information needs • Appropriate referrals • Policies and procedures • Evaluate collaborative efforts	Ability to assess user information needs: • Can apply subject headings to questions • Can write brief descriptions of questions • Can apply appropriate metadata • Can successfully route questions with all the required information • Can follow specified policies and procedures for collaborative conduct	Ability to successfully make higher-level triage and collaboration decisions: • Recognizes ques-tions suitable for referral • Applies appropriate criteria in selecting among multiple referral options • Understands strengths and weaknesses of collaborative partners	Ability to lead collaborative efforts and set triage and collaboration policies: • Can follow up to ensure that referred questions receive responses • Can work interactively with collaborators to schedule coverage and provide training • Can assess effectiveness of collaborative efforts

(Cont'd.)

Figure 9-37: Rubrics at a Glance *(Continued)*

COMPETENCY	BEGINNING: *skills focus*	INTERMEDIATE: *conceptual focus*	ADVANCED: *administrative focus*
Triage and Collaboration *(Cont'd.)*		• Recognizes question types and contextual factors affecting question handling • Recognizes underlying and unexpressed information needs	• Can make policy decisions regarding triage and collaboration • Can identify and pursue new opportunities for collaboration
Digital Reference Community Internal: • Understanding value of continuing education External: • Appreciation of wider community of digital reference services	• Seeks opportunities for continuing education • Develops knowledge of wider digital reference community through listservs, organizations, conferences, and networking	• Understands the value of continuing education as an agent for change • Contributes to the growth of digital reference field through participation in actual and virtual forums • Ability to understand how the wider community affects their local institution • Recommends new and different ways of approaching digital reference problems and concerns	• Provides encouragement and opportunities for the continuing education of staff • Actively supports digital reference collaborative efforts within and outside the institution • Actively contributes to the wider digital reference community through publications and presentations • Strives to implement new ways of solving problems and making the library a good place to work

(Cont'd.)

Figure 9-37: Rubrics at a Glance (Continued)			
COMPETENCY	BEGINNING: *skills focus*	INTERMEDIATE: *conceptual focus*	ADVANCED: *administrative focus*
Knowledge Base Acquisition and Use • Retain organizational knowledge • Reduce transaction time • Improve user satisfaction	• Awareness of resources created by colleagues through a database of questions and answers • Ability to use such resources created by colleagues	• Ability to evaluate appropriateness and efficacy of knowledge base resources • Awareness of policies governing knowledge base acquisition and use, and the ability to provide feedback on such policies	• Ability to plan and implement resource creation from data gathered from reference transactions • Demonstrates ability to use data mining techniques to refine or expand searches • Demonstrates ability to interpret data from knowledge base and apply findings to library services

Conclusion

Regular training in every aspect of library service is a desirable part of staff development. Though it is important to upgrade staff capabilities and knowledge to maintain a robust workforce and provide the best services and resources for patrons, ongoing training for virtual reference services is especially critical for an effective and high-quality reference department. Changes in technology, new and evolving electronic resources, and a technologically savvy clientele make for a challenging work environment. The demands of change and expectations of "instant" service can either encourage a climate that is creative and stimulating or beget one fraught with disenchantment and frustration. Ongoing competencies-based virtual reference training for existing and new staff members, as well as LIS students, will ensure a consistent level of proficiency and satisfaction in virtual reference service.

References

Berube, Linda. "Digital Reference Overview." Bath, UK: UKOLN (February 2003). Available: www.ukoln.ac.uk/public/nsptg/virtual/

Clark, Donald. "ISD Handbook." Edmonds, WA: Big Dog, Little Dog. (May 2006) Available: www.nwlink.com/~donclark/hrd/ sat.html

Horn, Judy. "The Future is Now: Reference Service for the Electronic Age." *ACRL 10th National Conference: Crossing the Divide, Denver, Colorado, March 15–18, 2001.* Chicago, IL: American Library Association (March 2001). Available: www.ala.org/ala/ acrl/acrlevents/horn.pdf

Janes, J. 2002. "Digital Reference: Reference Librarians' Experiences and Attitudes." *Journal of the American Society for Information Science and Technology* 53, no. 7: 549–566.

Lankes, R. D., and A. Kasowitz. 1998. *The AskA Starter Kit: How to Build and Maintain Digital Reference Services.* Syracuse, NY: ERIC Clearinghouse on Information & Technology.

Leveen, T. 2001. "Reference Librarians Chat It Up Online." *Today's Librarian* 4, no. 5: 17–19.

Lytle, S. L., and M. Wolfe. 1989. *Adult Literacy Education: Program Evaluation and Learner Assessment.* Columbus, OH: ERIC Clearinghouse on Adult, Career, and Vocational Education.

Massey-Burzio, V. 1992. "Reference Encounters of a Different Kind: A Symposium." *Journal of Academic Librarianship* 18, no. 5: 276–280.

McNamara, Carter. "Employee Training and Development: Reasons and Benefits." Minneapolis, MN: Free Management Library (1999). Available: www.management help.org/trng_dev/ basics/reasons.htm

Meola, M., and S. Stormont. 2002. *Starting and Operating Live Virtual Reference Services.* New York: Neal-Schuman.

Philbrick, Jodi, and Ana Cleveland. "A Model for Teaching Virtual Reference in a Virtual Classroom." Presentation at the 2005 VRD Conference in Burlingame, CA. Dublin: Online Computer Library Center (January 2006). Available: www.web-junction.org/do/DisplayContent; jsessionid=3F1D39D921C8AD26A74FF057896 862E2?id=12457

Ronan, Jana. "Chat Reference: An Exciting New Facet of Digital Reference Services." *ARL Bimonthly Report* 219. Washington, DC: Association of Research Libraries (December 2001). Available: www.arl.org/newsltr/219/chat.html

Salem, Joseph, Leela Balraj, and Erica Lilly. "Real-Time Training for Virtual Reference." Presentation at the 2003 VRD Conference in San Antonio, TX. Syracuse: Virtual Reference Desk (November 2003). Available: www.vrd.org/conferences/ VRD2003/proceedings/ presentation.cfm?PID=214

Wasik, Joann M. "Digital Reference Evaluation." Syracuse, NY: Virtual Reference Desk (June 2003). Available: www.vrd.org/AskA/ digref_assess.shtml

Index

(Items appearing in figures are marked with a letter 'f' following the page number)

About the Editors

R. David Lankes

R. David Lankes, Ph.D., is Director of the Information Institute of Syracuse (IIS) and an Associate Professor at Syracuse University's School of Information Studies. Lankes's past research projects include the Gateway to Educational Materials (GEM), the Virtual Reference Desk (VRD), and the Educator's Reference Desk. He is currently involved in projects related to the NSF's National Science Digital Library (NSDL) and several IMLS studies. Lankes was director of the ERIC Clearinghouse on Information & Technology (1998–2003) and co-founded the award-winning AskERIC project in 1992. He was a visiting scholar to Harvard's Graduate School of Education and a visiting fellow at the National Library of Canada.

Philip Nast

Philip Nast is a freelance writer. He has worked for ERIC, Department of Education, GEM, AskNSDL, VRD, and Roads from Seneca Falls. He writes every month for PBS's *TeacherSource* and *Get Local*. A former middle school teacher, his past projects have included resource materials for middle school social studies textbooks. He received an MFA from Syracuse University and a BA in English from Marietta College.

Scott Nicholson

Dr. Scott Nicholson is an Assistant Professor at the School of Information Studies and a research scientist for the Information Institute of Syracuse at Syracuse University. His primary research area is the measurement and evaluation of digital library services through bibliomining, or the combination of data mining, bibliometrics, statistics, and reporting tools used to extract patterns of behavior-based artifacts from library systems. He has worked as a reference librarian for Texas Christian University and as a statistician for Citigroup, and combines these backgrounds in his research and teaching. Dr. Nicholson's other research interests include Web search tools and community building in distance education.

Marie L. Radford

Marie L. Radford is an Associate Professor at Rutgers University, SCILS. Prior to this, she was Acting Dean and Associate Professor at Pratt Institute's School of Information and Library Science. She holds a Ph.D. in Communication, Information & Library Science (Rutgers) and an MSLS (Syracuse). Prior to arriving at Pratt in 1996, she was Head of Curriculum Materials at the William Paterson University of N.J. Cheng Library. Her research interests are interpersonal aspects of reference service (in traditional and virtual environments), evaluation of e-resources and services, cultural studies, and media stereotypes of librarians. She makes frequent presentations at national and international communication and library conferences and has published in *College & Research Libraries, Library Quarterly, Library Trends, JELIS, JASIST*, and the *Journal of Academic Librarianship*. Her books include: *The Reference Encounter: Interpersonal Communication in the Academic Library* (ACRL/ALA, 1999) and *Web Research: Selection, Evaluation, and Citing* (Allyn & Bacon, 2002; 2nd ed., 2006). Active in the ALA, she is past chair of the Library Research Round Table and a member of the ALA Research & Statistics Committee and the RUSA/MOUSS Publications Committee. Her Web site is www.scils.rutgers.edu/~mradford and she blogs at Library Garden: http://librarygarden.blogspot.com/

Joanne Silverstein

Joanne L. Silverstein, Ph.D., is Director of Research & Development of the Information Institute of Syracuse (IIS) and an Assistant Research Professor at Syracuse University's School of Information Studies. Dr. Silverstein conducts research into the evolving role of human intermediation in Web-based information provision for education and library-related use. She has published on the topics of children's informal learning and their use of digital reference services. Her current projects include a meta-library for women's history (Roads From Seneca Falls) and science education resources for children (Students Using the National Science Digital Library or SUN).

Lynn Westbrook

Lynn Westbrook has a dozen years as an academic reference/instruction librarian and a decade as an LIS faculty member. With an MLS from University of Chicago and a Ph.D. from University of Michigan (Ann Arbor), she has published two books and over 20 articles on information seeking, user needs, and research methods. Her current research centers on mental models of information seeking, information support for domestic violence survivors, and communication patterns in chat reference.

About the Contributors

Lisa Ancelet

Lisa Ancelet is the Virtual Reference Services Librarian, Albert B. Alkek Library, Texas State University–San Marcos. In her current position, Lisa is responsible for the majority of the VR hours offered by the Ask a Librarian Live service and is one of 12 reference librarians participating in virtual reference. Her other duties include monitoring virtual reference services, in addition to staffing the main reference desk and conducting library instruction sessions. Lisa earned her MS in Information Studies at the University of Texas at Austin in 2003, and her BA in History from McNeese State University in 1995.

Jean Ferguson

Jean Ferguson is a Reference Librarian and Coordinator of Virtual Reference at the Perkins Bostock Library at Duke University. She has an MLS from UNC in Chapel Hill, North Carolina, an MS from Ball State University in Muncie, Indiana, and a BA from Augustana College in Rock Island, Illinois. Jean has been at Duke since 2004.

Lorin Flores Fisher

Lorin Flores Fisher is a Reference/Instruction Librarian at the Alkek Library, Texas State University–San Marcos. In addition to conducting library instruction sessions, she participates actively in virtual reference and served as Virtual Reference Pilot Project Coordinator during the initial implementation phase. She also has worked on other projects exploring new uses for technology in the library. She earned her MLS degree from the University of North Texas and also holds a BA in English and Spanish from Texas State University–San Marcos.

Helene Lafrance

Helene Lafrance is currently Head of Research Assistance at the Orradre Library, as well as the library liaison for the Social Sciences. She has been the Virtual Reference Coordinator for Santa Clara University since 2002 and served as Co-Chair of the AJCU Virtual Reference Implementation Committee.

A native of Quebec, Canada, Helene received a BA and a MA in French Literature from the Universite de Sherbrooke in 1983 and a Master of Library and Information Science from UC Berkeley in 1990.

Jack Maness

Jack Maness is Engineering Reference and Instruction Librarian at the Gemmill Engineering Library, University of Colorado at Boulder. Prior to coming to the university, Maness was Librarian at Remington College in Lakewood, Colorado, and held many positions at the Denver Public Library. He has provided virtual reference at all three institutions. Maness holds a Master of Library Science from Emporia State University and a Bachelor of Arts in English Literature from the University of Colorado at Denver.

Locke Morrisey

Locke Morrisey has been the head of the Reference & Research Services Department at the University of San Francisco's (USF) Gleeson Library/Geschke Learning Resource Center since October 1997 and Coordinator of Collections since October 2000. He is also the library liaison to the School of Nursing and departments of Biology and Chemistry. Prior to coming to USF, he served as Engineering Librarian at the University of California, Irvine (1990–1997), and as a librarian at Hughes Aircraft Electro-Optical and Data Systems Group Technical Library (1987–1990). Locke received a BA in Biology from UCLA in 1979 and a Master of Library Science from UCLA in 1986.

Sarah Naper

Sarah Naper is a Business Reference Librarian at the University of Northern Colorado's James A. Michener Library in Greeley, Colorado. Naper previously worked as a Government Documents and Reference Librarian at North Harris College in Houston, Texas and in Houston Public Library's Business, Science, and Technology department. Naper holds a Master of Science in Library Science, University of North Texas, and a Bachelor of Arts in English, University of Texas.

Clara Ogbaa

Dr. Clara Ogbaa is the Head of Reference & Instructional Services at the Alkek Library, Texas State University–San Marcos. She provided the leadership for the implementation of virtual reference service at Texas State University and was instrumental in getting the service off the ground. She is responsible for the overall planning, direction, coordination and supervision of all reference activities. She has extensive experience training, and presenting on effective reference performance, conducts staff training, and coordinates the VRS scheduling. She holds a doctorate degree in Educational Leadership from the University of Bridgeport in Connecticut, and an MLIS and BA in English from The University of Texas at Austin.

Debbie Rabina

Debbie Rabina is an Assistant Professor at Pratt Institute-SILS. Her areas of research and teaching are in reference sources and services and in information policy. Reference areas of expertise include general reference, government documents, and information sources in the humanities and social sciences. Dr. Rabina teaching and research focus on the strong interactions between the humanities and computers, as well as on the increasing importance of scholarly communications for the reference librarian.

Gabriel R. Rios

Gabriel R. Rios is Deputy Director of the Lister Hill Library of the Health Sciences at the University of Alabama at Birmingham. Previously, he was Associate Director for Public Services at the University of Texas Health Science Center San Antonio Libraries, where he directed the Public Services Division of the UTHSCSA Libraries and was also responsible for managing library services of satellite libraries, including the UTHSCSA Regional Academic Health Center, the Brady Green Library, and the Laredo Extension Campus Library. In current and previous positions, Rios provided leadership and vision for key public services, including reference services, Web presence, education programs, liaison programs, outreach services, and information technology. Rios has coordinated and provided virtual and in-person reference services in many environments, including academic medical centers, hospitals, and community health centers. Rios received his BA in Anthropology from the University of Texas at San Antonio and his MLIS from the University of Texas at Austin.

Pam Sessoms

Pam Sessoms is the Electronic Reference Services Librarian for the Davis Library, University of North Carolina at Chapel Hill, and coordinates the VR services in the Reference Department. She has a BA and an MLS from UNC–Chapel Hill and has been with the reference department since 1994.

Catherine Arnott Smith

Catherine Arnott Smith is an Assistant Professor in the School of Library and Information Studies, University of Wisconsin–Madison. She was formerly an Assistant Professor at the School of Information Studies, Syracuse University (2002–2006). Arnott Smith was formerly a medical reference librarian at Northwestern University and an information systems developer at Lincoln National Reinsurance Companies. From 1997 to 2002, she was a full-time NLM predoctoral fellow at the Center for Biomedical Informatics at the University of Pittsburgh, where she worked on a multimedia electronic medical record system; her ssertation was the first to examine the Clinical Document Architecture, a new 'L standard for medical record exchange in health care. Her work focuses on erface between consumers and the electronic medical record, and she has nded by the Medical Library Association, IBM's Center for Healthcare ent, and the National Historic and Public Records Commission.

Judy Trump

At the time of writing, Judy Trump was Head of the Government Documents and Microforms Department at Georgetown University's Lauinger Library. She served as Government Documents Reference Librarian (1997–2006), and was the Virtual Reference Coordinator at Georgetown from 2000 until 2006. She served as Co-Chair of the AJCU Virtual Reference Steering Committee. Judy received a BA in French from Albright College in 1975, and a Master of Library and Information Science from The Catholic University of America in 1996.

Joann Wasik

Joann Wasik is currently a freelance researcher and book indexer. She served as a Research Consultant & Communications Officer for the Virtual Reference Desk (VRD) Project (1998–2005), and Project Manager for The Digital Reference Education Initiative (DREI) from 2003 until 2006. Her previous experience also includes technology training and positions in academic libraries. Joann holds BA and MAT degrees in English from Boston College, and an MLS degree from Syracuse University.